Kirk,
You're a big
I love the
of god and others.

Ed Jones
Daniel 10:18-19

UP AGAINST THE WALL

Edwin Jones

UP AGAINST THE WALL

Tall and True Tales from West Berlin,
the Island City

TATE PUBLISHING
AND ENTERPRISES, LLC

Up Against the Wall
Copyright © 2013 by Edwin Jones. All rights reserved.

No part of this publication may be reproduced, stored in a retrieval system or transmitted in any way by any means, electronic, mechanical, photocopy, recording or otherwise without the prior permission of the author except as provided by USA copyright law.

The opinions expressed by the author are not necessarily those of Tate Publishing, LLC.

Published by Tate Publishing & Enterprises, LLC
127 E. Trade Center Terrace | Mustang, Oklahoma 73064 USA
1.888.361.9473 | www.tatepublishing.com

Tate Publishing is committed to excellence in the publishing industry. The company reflects the philosophy established by the founders, based on Psalm 68:11, *"The Lord gave the word and great was the company of those who published it."*

Book design copyright © 2013 by Tate Publishing, LLC. All rights reserved.
Cover design by Rtor Maghuyop
Interior design by Joana Quilantang

Published in the United States of America

ISBN: 978-1-62510-720-6
1. Biography & Autobiography / General
2. Biography & Autobiography / Military
13.02.20

Edie, my wife and mentor, helped correct and edit the draft. She inspired me to keep my writing intentional rather than haphazard, a definite temptation when many of the tales are so humorous or ridiculous. I am in her debt and that of our Creator who saved us both after these incidents were but memories.

TABLE OF CONTENTS

Introduction -- 9
Prologue -- 11
First Impressions -- 15
Shots in the Dark, Our First Night ---------------------------------- 25
Troika -- 33
A Pair of Shorts and a Long --- 43
We Called Him Prince Jim -- 55
Perspective --- 61
Party Central --- 85
Nerves of Steel at the Helm --- 91
Edie Forges East Berlin --- 97
Berlin, the "Island City" -- 105
Encounters -- 123
BWPSBBBT, Bowling for Buses -------------------------------------- 135
What Type of Ice Cream Do You Like with Your Hijacking? ------ 141
Pirate Invasion --- 151
Runaway Tank -- 159
Gruppenreisen --- 169
A Piece of the Wall -- 187
Epilogue -- 193
Endnotes --- 197

INTRODUCTION

Have you grown weary of insider tell-all books? You know the ones I mean. They reveal every action, every nuance of protocol, procedure, and actual workings within this or that secret organization? I know I have. Further, I'm no longer enamored with whistle-blowers. It seems to me that so many have emerged as of late that nothing seems to be sacred or sacrosanct. There have been so many books written in this genre that I believe most are simply ignored. The writer's motives may be pure, but one tends to assume that the motive of each expose is money or an attempt to break free from a life of anonymity.

What follows is not a tell-all. As a matter of fact, it's quite the opposite. It's merely a compendium of stories and vignettes I picked up or took part in while living in Berlin. Yes, I speak Russian. Yes, I was assigned to a couple of signals intelligence units in Berlin. Yes, I taught at NSA. No, I was nothing special. I'm just one of thousands of men and women with similar skills, experiences, and background.

Reminisces and stories in this book occurred during the first two decades that the Berlin Wall stood. They represent what happens when men and women who are otherwise reasonably intelligent decide to take leave of those senses and buck the system. They also depict the extreme disdain we had for the East Germans and Soviets who chose to wall in and enslave a population to prop up an ideology that was doomed to failure.

As the title indicates, I cannot vouch for the veracity of all the stories I've detailed. Many of these had already passed into legend by the time I arrived in 1970. I'm more certain of details in those adventures in which I took part, but time and age have dulled and sometimes obscured specifics.

It should be noted that I've changed the names of everyone who might still be alive except my wife and me. I didn't want anyone still living to be associated with the outlandish anecdotes herein related.

The chapters follow no particular chronology, nor does their location indicate relative importance of one over another. I have not attempted to intersperse them in relation to their level of humor or seriousness. So, sit back and enjoy my memories of the town and those who worked to defend it.

PROLOGUE

I enlisted in the U.S. Air Force in November 1966. I was attempting to enroll in Utica College after graduating from Hudson Valley Community College, Troy, New York. The loan officer called to inform me my loan papers had been mislaid and that they had to notify the draft board. About a week later, I was classified 1A, and given the time and situation of the war, prepared for the inevitable. I was indeed drafted by the U.S. Army, but through some quick and probably "less-than-kosher" action by the air force recruiter, I was able to opt for blue rather than green garb. A subsequent skiing accident kept me from reporting for basic training at Lackland AFB until February of 1967.

During basic, I happened to pass a linguistic exam that, according to the examiners, only one or two in one hundred passed. The test was a made-up language based on Latin, French, and Slavic languages. Since I had spoken some Polish as a child and had taken Latin and French in high school, I'm sure I had an advantage. At any rate, after graduating from basic training, I was held over at Lackland until a class could be formed. Currently, linguists are trained at the Defense Language Institute at Monterey, California with some training taking place at service locations. In my day, the military contracted with various colleges throughout the U.S. to train their linguists. I was assigned to a basic Russian class at a compound called Skytop on the grounds of Syracuse University.

The three linguistics plateaus one could negotiate then were basic, intermediate, and advanced programs. Each program lasted nine months and was conducted with near total immersion in the language. My instructors were all defectors from the former Soviet Union, and each bore the emotional and physical scars of encounters with the KGB. They sported names such as

Ubans, Wurtilevski, Protopopov, Ermaluk, Gan, Bultunova, and Stennin. They were strict and disciplined and objects of great awe among the student body. They were also predictable, adhering to what we named the Slavic emotional grading system. Simply, their first impression of our abilities or lack thereof seemed to determine our final grade. To test our premise, members of my advanced Russian class at the Defense Language Institute Foreign Language Center (DLIFLC), Monterey, California, guessed what our final grades would be based on teacher's comments and level of appreciation for our work. Each of us wrote these numbers on a three by five card and taped them underneath our homeroom desk drawer. We did this during the second week of the nine-month program. Amazingly, each prediction save one came true. The one in error was off by two points. If memory serves right, my grade was ninety-two.

Syracuse was, in a word, wonderful. We learned linguistics, literature, economics, political science, and geography. We even learned to buy common staples and cook special holiday meals. We were treated to Soviet propaganda films from the 1950s and all the works of the incredible Sergei Eisenstein. We had daily dictations, memorizations, and were expected to carry on complete conversations within three months. When not studying and visiting our favorite watering hole, the Poor House East with its floor covered in peanut shells, I traveled home. My family lived in Albany, New York, which is some 140 miles from Syracuse. I was then dating my wife-to-be and spent the majority of my money and spare time on Greyhound buses.

After graduation, we were all assigned to Goodfellow Air Force Base, San Angelo, Texas, for technical training in the art of signals and communications intelligence. The three-month program introduced us to the world of electronic intelligence gathering for the National Security Agency, an institution that would later allow me to instruct several programs at their cryptologic school in 1974–1978. After graduation and a third promotion, I traveled home to marry my sweetheart, Edie. I arrived on a Thursday, was married two days later on Saturday, traveled to Hampton Beach, New Hampshire for a two-week honeymoon, and left alone for my next assignment when we returned to Albany.

I was posted to Wakkanai Air Station (WAS), Wakkanai, Japan. It was on the northern tip of Hokkaido, as far north as you can go in Japan without getting your feet wet. The unit had various designations over its lifetime, but it was mostly the 6986th Security Group, a unit of the late, great USAF Security Service. Wakkanai was a surveillance site, with a (then) state-of-the-art system known as a FLR-12. The FLR-12 had a huge antenna farm. Wakkanai opened in the mid-1950s as an aircraft control and warning (AC&W) radar site; it ceased operations in late 1971 and closed in 1972. I was there in 1968 and 1969. The tour was designated isolated because of its remote location. I had yet to reenlist, so I was not authorized to travel accompanied. In other words, the military would not pay for my wife's travel, and we would not be provided housing. The length of such a tour was fifteen months. We decided to save our pennies, and Edie joined me in December on a visa that we had to renew twice. She stayed for six months.

I remember that our marriage caused quite a stir since Edie's birth city was Lima, Peru. Upon arrival, I was assigned to the orderly room for a couple of weeks while the FBI checked out her family to make sure my clearance was secure.

The one thing people always remember about Wakkanai is the snow and the constant wind. We had an average annual snow fall of 275 inches. You can do the math—that's a tick shy of twenty-three feet of snow every year. And it was cold. And the wind blew constantly and with such force that Edie was knocked off her feet on base one day. The snow began to fall in earnest in late November and stayed on the ground until late March or early April. While I was there, snow remained well into May.

All of the bases were surrounded with at least eight-foot-high chain-link fences, usually topped with three strands of barbed wire. In midwinter, the fences at WAS were useless. Even though it was illegal to leave the base through anything but the main gate (and if you got caught you were in trouble!), we routinely scrambled up and down the snow banks that obscured the fence and went "across the street." "Across the street" was a euphemism for the three dive bars that were literally across the street from the base—Club Seven, Inferno, and Shadow. Further down was my favorite, the Chidori. Mama-san sure could make some great pork fried rice and niwatori (chicken kebobs). I ran a monthly tab at the Chidori—it was a welcome change from the chow hall.

There wasn't a lot to do in the winter. Private vehicles weren't allowed on the roads in the winter, so we became semi-isolated, except for busses or taxis into town. We worked, partied, worked. Rinse. Repeat. Having Edie there for six months was more than a blessing. We walked in the snow and wind and saw approximately twenty movies each month. When she left, I moved back into the barracks.

I returned home to a wife, a beautiful daughter, Chantelle Marie, and another assignment to Syracuse DLI for Intermediate Russian Language. I began in January, 1970, and we found an apartment on James Street. After graduation, I went to West Berlin, and Edie and Chantelle went back to Albany. In Albany, Edie gave birth to our son, Darby Lee. She would have to travel to Berlin with a one-month-old infant and a thirteen-month-old toddler. In that move, she displayed courage I never had.

In Berlin, during 1970–74 and again, in 1978–81, the chapters that follow came into being.

FIRST IMPRESSIONS

It was 1970, and I had just taken off from Frankfurt. I stared through the tiny airplane window, looking down as free West Germany disappeared. *Huh*, I thought, *it doesn't look any different than the farms in upstate New York*. I was looking at the much talked about air corridor into Berlin. Mildly amused and yet unnerved at the same time, I wondered what I was supposed to see now that I was behind the Iron Curtain.

Berlin. That's where I was headed, the walled city. I didn't know what to expect, but I had been told there was no other assignment like it. Of course, I had been told the same thing about my last assignment, Wakkanai, Japan. The ubiquitous "they" hadn't been far from wrong then. Wakkanai was a small fishing village jutting out into the La Perouse Straight on the far northern tip of the island Hokkaido. I still couldn't believe the snow, two hundred and fifty plus inches during my last winter there. Cold, barely habitable, I had managed to make the best of the assignment and had developed a reputation there for doing good work. There had been plenty of work to do with Soviet-owned Sakhalin Island visible on a clear day. I imagined that the work in Berlin would be no less exciting and challenging. What I did not, could not, know was that Wakkanai was only a prelude and that Berlin would be a turning point in my life.

As the plane descended into West Berlin, I strained to make out shapes and forms. Farmland gave way to habitation, and I could see the bustle of my new home for the next several years. I saw "the wall" and wondered what it would be like living on an island, as Berlin was referred to. I then caught sight of Tempelhof Zentral Flughafen or Tempelhof Central Airport–TCA. It did resemble an eagle with its wings stretched out and up. The landing was a gut-tightener, as the plane came in between the buildings and literally dropped onto the runway. As it came to a halt near the great canopy that greeted visitors, I could make out a thin, wiry staff sergeant waiting at the window of the reception area. *That has to be Ted*, I murmured to myself.

Ted and I hit it off immediately. This was a good thing, since he would be my constant companion during the critical first few days of acquaintance and acclimation. While we waited for luggage, Ted made it clear that my immediate concern in the walled city was to learn my job. To the novice, shift work offered little time for anything other than eating, working, and sleeping. Shift work, I had found out in Wakkani, was a euphemism for prolonged suicide. At a typical site, four flights worked shift, each duplicating the work of the other with three shifts on duty at all times while the other was on break. It operated like this; a shift would come off break and work four successive swings from 4:00 p.m. to midnight. After the last swing, they would have twenty-four hours off and then work four successive mids, which ran from midnight to 8:00 a.m. Again, they would have twenty-four hours to recoup and prepare for four "day watches" which ran from 8:00 a.m. to 4:00 p.m. They would then be given ninety-six hours off (four full days) and begin the cycle again. It was merciless. Circadian rhythm was unknown to those on shift. And many, like me, worked this crazy schedule for years. My sweet wife, Edie, would eventually refer to it as "our seventeen-day-week." People who worked this bizarre schedule not only forgot birthdays and anniversaries, they would be hard-pressed to tell you what month it was, let alone what day. Nonetheless, I looked forward to my new duties, duties officially designated as a Russian linguist and translator, at the U.S. Air Force signals intelligence site at Marienfelde, which practically butted up against the infamous Berlin Wall.

After I retrieved my baggage, Ted and I made our way to base and the CQ to sign in and get a room assignment. Thus, began the arduous and time-consuming task of settling into a new assignment. Over the course of the next several days, I attended welcome briefings from the commander, first sergeant, and myriad lesser luminaries. I completed endless forms and acquired the all-important picture badge, color coded to signify type of clearance and access. My final act of acclimation after I got my postal box was to pick up my gas mask. This would prove useful during my semi-annual gassing to prepare us for possible hostilities with the Soviets and East Germans. *Great, just great,* I thought, *in the unlikely event that the Russians ever attack us with tear gas, I'm prepared and protected!*

My assigned room was on the third floor above hangar three at Tempelhof. In spite of the fact that it was on the third floor room, it seemed subterranean. The hall was gloomy and dank, and the room appeared as dark as night. The only window in the room looked into the immense, dingy hangar. To add to the ambiance, my temporary roommate, Sergeant Simon Pavel, chain-smoked Turkish and East European cigarettes. The acrid cloud they created in the confined space gave me a new reason to appreciate the recently acquired gas mask. This gave me added impetus to get an apartment and soon, before my roommate's brown cigarettes killed me.

On the breaks from duty, it was standard procedure for Charlie Flight to hang out together. Some drank a lot, and some just came along for the show. A bunch of the guys I would be working with were recouping from their last mid at Club Silverwings, the Noncommissioned Officers Club–the NCO Club–and they all wanted to meet the "jeep" (air force term for "new kid on the block").

"This is our NCO Club," Ted proudly announced as we ascended the steep granite steps. "Hope you have some money, because you're expected to buy a round or two." The club was larger and more lavish than I had anticipated. It far surpassed the close quarters of the club in Wakkanai with its bank of slot machines lining the wall in front of the bar.

"Ah, there they are," Ted said as he motioned to the assembled troops. "C'mon, they're all waiting to meet you."

I was greeted with a chorus of boos and jeers as I approached the guys with whom I'd be working for the next few years.

"Hey man, how's it going?" offered the short, pudgy man with an engaging smile. "I'm Ralph Logan, but everyone calls me Animal. Here, let me introduce you. You're Ed, right?" I nodded. "Damn, 'Ed' just ain't gonna cut it. Let's see—you're a right strappin' young fella." Ralph said in a good imitation of a farm boy accent. "Have you ever been on a horse?" I nodded again, somewhat puzzled at the question. "All right! Everyone has to have a nickname and we're going to call you Cowboy. Where are you from in the States?"

"New York," I replied with a smirk.

"Don't matter. Ain't gonna change your name just because you've never lived west of Manhattan. Just don't tell anyone," Animal snickered. He pointed lazily with his drink to the man on his left. "This is Phil Leggett, but we call him Reptile. You'll be sitting rack next to him after you side-saddle with Ted for a shift."

I took in the faces around him. These were the men and women that I would work with and, so it appeared, with whom would spend many off duty hours. They weren't shy in talking about themselves. Animal was from Indiana. He grew up on a farm and, according to him, spent more time in the barn than in the house, hence the nickname. Apparently, Animal was already a legend mainly due to his vulgarity in word and deed. Those who knew him well would remark that the fact that Animal maintained his security clearance was one of the great mysteries of the Cold War. Bereft of moral compass, his saving grace was his phenomenal intellect and disarming humor. He was a "reporter" on flight. As I would soon discover, Animal spent his spare time devising ways to gross out those with whom he worked.

Reptile was artistic and loud, about five foot nine with a shock of sandy hair topping a slightly puffy face. Leggett hailed from Wyoming. He was also a linguist and, according to him, a good one. His abilities were such that he did seem to occupy a place of some esteem among the members of Charlie Flight, my new family. As predicted, we would work side-by-side and he would be instrumental in expanding my arrest record while in West Berlin. The logbook that he and I were required to maintain was full of our artwork. Reptile was a master of the then-popular psychedelic style of art. He and Animal were best friends and single; they spent endless off-duty hours together in ardent debauch.

The others at the table were Ronnie Tinker, the mission supervisor for Charlie. Fortyish, with twenty plus years of service, Ronnie was nearing retirement. Hard to ruffle, easy going, a good ear for languages, he often would help the other linguists and enjoyed keeping his hand in.

Downing the better part of a tumbler of straight bourbon, Lowell Walker, L.W., to his friends, jumped to his feet and vigorously shook my hand. "Glad to meet you, you'll fit in just fine. Isn't it time you buy a round?" As I fumbled for my wallet, I sized up this new acquaintance. Lowell was about five feet eleven with an unremarkable face. He wore maroon polyester pants, a yellow polo shirt, which matched his socks, grey hush puppies, and a maroon jacket with Udorn, Thailand embroidered above a garish flying dragon completely covering the back of the jacket. As I would discover later, Lowell was hyper and knew only one speed, full. Lowell was also a reporter but of a different type than Animal. Next to Lowell sat a tall, statuesque young woman, Lana Eckert. Although she was not beautiful, she was striking. Barefoot, she was six feet even. When in heels, she towered over most of the men on her flight. She was a German linguist, which made her even more popular with Charlie Flight, most of whom knew only English and Russian or no foreign language at all. She was very open about her unlucky streak in relationships and had been married at least twice. Like her male counterparts, (very few women were allowed into the command at the time) she seemed to be on the lunatic fringe while trying to maintain some sense of decorum. As it turned out much to my surprise, she was Ted's roommate along with another young woman, Lacy. Ted was just full of surprises.

As others on the flight straggled in to join the fun, I was compelled to buy them a round also. As the evening wore on, I learned quite a bit about my mates. Each of them had unique personality traits that promised to make our hours at work anything but boring. I could see that off-duty hours were going to be eventful and maybe just a little reckless. For some reason, the recklessness appealed to the daredevil in me.

I stayed much later than I should have and dreaded the long walk back to the room. I made my way down an endless hallway back to the dorm room wondering what my first day at work would be like.

The short break between mids and days was over. This was the first day watch. The early morning found the crew waiting for the bus to Marienfelde. As I scanned TCA, I wondered if anyone had ever seen every square foot of the immense building that stretched for the better part of mile in each direction. I'd heard rumors that there were several floors underground that were off limits to all. Someone mentioned something about an aircraft assembly area hastily constructed towards the end of WWII, then torched and flooded by the Soviets during their liberation of the city. Animal caught me staring at one of the entrances to the subterranean tomb.

"There's still Nazis down there," he offered. "The Russkies didn't want to mess with going below the first or second levels, so they used flame throwers to soften up the opposition and then dumped a few million gallons of water into the hole. No one is allowed down there."

As soon as Animal said no one was allowed down there, I knew I'd have to see for myself someday.

The big blue Mercedes bus careened up the steep ramp from the motor pool. "Mercedes?" Until now, I'd only heard of that name associated with the super expensive and luxurious automobiles. I didn't even know they made other vehicles, let alone busses. "Such luxury. Must be a wonderful ride," I commented. "Right," replied Reptile sarcastically. I soon discovered the reason for the curt reply. The springs under the seats resembled pig iron rather than spring steel. With its passengers safely aboard, the bus driver sped out of the gate and into Berlin traffic, the ruts and ridges in the cobblestone roads jarred my teeth with every bump. I now understood Reptile's comment. "Whoa! Have the Mercedes people ridden these buses? If this is a Mercedes, give me a Volkswagen," I managed to ground out between bumps.

The city was alive, and I took in every sight, sound and smell as the bus made the turn onto Columbiadamm. "There's Snoopy's," someone shouted as the bus passed a bar frequented by the flight. "We'll introduce to you its charms this break," added another. The ride was uneventful, even without proper springs. The city gave way to farmland and forest as the bus made endless twists and turns. *How am I supposed to remember how to get here from the new apartment?* I wondered.

"There she is!" someone announced. As the bus passed a stand of conifers, the site at Marienfelde came into view. High atop a man-made mountain constructed of the rubble left after endless allied bombing missions and Russian destruction, the conglomeration of buildings and bubbles resembled something created by Rod Serling for the "Twilight Zone." They seemed to be connected haphazardly with little concern for form or function. Amazed and somewhat intimidated at the sight, I remember thinking that a two-year-old must have designed this place. Towers that looked like the result of an Erector Set experiment gone awry stuck out from every conceivable location. They jutted up from several roofs and from the landscape surrounding the mishmash of buildings. Atop these engineering marvels were the largest golf balls I had ever seen. The dimpled white skin resembling golf balls actually served as protection for an endless array of antennas. I was soon to learn their use.

Up the steep road that doubled as a ski slope in the winter, the bus strained for the first time. Finally, the Mercedes came to a stop and fatigue-clad soldiers clambered out into the morning sun.

"It's not so bad here," I blurted.

"Just wait," answered Animal.

In front of us stood our place of work surrounded by wire, sensors and spirals of razor wire. The exterior of the buildings didn't appear to deserve such deliberate attention. The guard shack that protected the entry gate appeared no larger than a British phone booth. Flashing badges, members of Charlie Flight began to make their way past the shack and through the gate in single file. I was disappointed with the apparent ease of entry. I thought it would be a bit more demanding. I hadn't counted on the security guard inside the door. As I entered a small building jutting out from a larger one, I noticed a few dozen holes running up the side of one of the walls. I shot a quizzical look at Reptile.

"Oh, that. Not to worry. A couple of weeks ago one of the gate guards went a little south on us, put his M-16 on auto and took out his frustration on the building," replied Reptile indifferently. "They work shift too, and I guess the combination of isolation and lack of sleep finally moved his bubble off of center. They plan to fill the holes while we're on break. Actually, he did us a favor– the whole damn place needs a paint job."

"What happened to him?" I asked .

"Aw, the 'disoriented express' picked him up. We'll never see him again. He'll never see his clearance or Berlin again."

After entering, I encountered the second gate guard who once again checked my badge against his display screen, presumably with information about me depicted. The hallway to operations was long and painted a depressing green. *I thought we were in the air force*, I mumbled as I took in the uninspired army olive drab green color. Once actually in operations, I met the rest of the flight. There were thirty-nine airmen and women representing numerous Air Force Specialty Codes (AFSCs). After the introductions, I was given a tour of the facility including the position, or rack, I would be riding for the next three years.

It was during my tour that I met my supervisor. At first encounter, Fielding Trainor was different than the remainder of the team, notwithstanding his forty-two years. Although dark brown hair still remained, it had already been invaded by ever widening streaks of gray. Mustachioed, his face was clean-shaven as were the rest of the flight. But there was something other than age that set him apart from the rest. Simply, it was his manner. First of all, Fielding spoke with polysyllabic words and didn't replace punctuation with expletives, as did his comrades. Although I could cuss with the best of them, I never understood why seemingly intelligent people "dumbed down" and resorted to gross vulgarity when communicating one with another. I too enjoyed using the vocabulary I had been taught, and this initial discussion with Fielding was refreshing. Second, Fielding fancied himself somewhat of an intellectual and Renaissance man. While this should have turned me off, Fielding presented himself with such grace and good humor as to make this affected personality intriguing rather than annoying. All in all, I liked the man. We would become friends.

Later that evening at the club, I asked, "So, tell me about Berlin. What's it like here?" The resulting barrage of stories, real and embellished, captured my attention for the better part of three liters of Berliner Kindl. Each person had a favorite tale of mischief, mayhem and misadventure, each trying to better the previous story. A few of the stories caught my imagination. Their veracity would have been sworn to upon a stack of Bibles, if such a stack had been present. Even if they weren't true, I thought they were the stuff of legend.

SHOTS IN THE DARK, OUR FIRST NIGHT

Our first home was in the Zehlendorf District of West Berlin. At the time, December 1970, the complex was still under construction. We were the first residents of the apartment. I had PCS (Permanent Change of Duty Station, which translates to a major move) in November. During that time, I'd secured travel for Edie, accommodations for my family, and started training for my new position at Marienfelde. I'd also moved into the dorm, that oppressive room with a window that opened into one of the hangars at Tempelhof Central Airport. I was very anxious for my family to arrive.

It took much less time to acclimate to the environment than it had in Japan. For the most part, the Germans were grateful for our presence, and although I had yet to learn the language, I could at least recognize the letters. When out of uniform, we were much more able to...blend into the crowd. I spent much of my free time learning my job and my new environment while preparing for the arrival of my family. Although we had been married more than two years, this would be our first real home. We were married in July 1968. Immediately upon return from our honeymoon, I caught a plane for Japan. Edie didn't join me until December. Our apartment there was small and made for a people several inches shorter than us. We were never sure if the authorities would renew Edie's sixty-day visa. They did once, so Edie left after six months. When she left, she was five months pregnant. When I returned to Albany, Edie and our daughter Chantelle were living at her mom and dad's house. They stayed there until I got accommodations in Syracuse where I was attending my second nine-month language school, intermediate Russian. We had a very tiny place on James Street and lived there for only seven months. Our son, Darby, was born 366 days after our daughter. I left Edie in New York and traveled to Berlin. In a very real sense, we would finally start our life together with two children. We were anxious to be a family.

I picked Edie up at Tegel Airport in the French sector. She and the children had traveled on Pan Am 1, the famous round-the-world flight that left JFK late every evening. They had changed planes in Dublin, Ireland and were exhausted when they finally landed. I still marvel at the trip she made with a toddler and baby. It took more courage than I possess. The long cab ride back to the apartment was a time to get reacquainted and to attempt to explain what the apartment would be like. I had no real point of reference. Our apartment in Wakkanai was a dump compared to this one.

The apartment was on the seventh floor. When she entered, Edie's fatigue was gone. The German government had provided it and all of the furnishings to include china and silverware. We were still an occupying force, a fact that authorized me to wear the WWII Army of Occupation Medal. As such, the Germans funded everything to do with our protection of West Berlin. I'll let Edie describe it in her own words, which follow:

> Having spent fourteen hours traveling with a one-month old and a thirteen-month old, we finally arrived in Berlin. Ed met us looking quite handsome in his blue blazer, and took us to what looked to me to be a palace after all those hours on the plane! It was 4 Charles H King Strasse, a brand new seventh floor apartment, complete with a balcony. We were the first tenants in the brand new apartment.
>
> Entering through the foyer, the large, even by American standards, kitchen was on the right, complete with Rosenthal china for twelve, heavy hotel silverware, and

all the pots and pans anyone could ever need, all courtesy o f the West Germans for us to use while we're there. There were lots of clean white cabinets, counters, drawers, a European stove, and a large fridge. Ah, it was a nice change from the Japanese kitchen I'd dealt with before. To the left, down the short hall was a double coat closet, phone, intercom to the downstairs entrance door, then a powder room. The living-dining room was very spacious, with floor-to-ceiling windows along one side overlooking a children's playground and park and apartment buildings beyond. Farther on was what looked like a forest; in reality it disguised part of The Wall.

The apartment was furnished with Swedish modern furniture with an Oriental rug over the tiled floors. Three bedrooms led off a hall from the living room, each with a built-in closet/drawers spanning one wall, so there was no need for dressers. Large windows in each had heavy draperies that blocked out every speck of light, which was great for sleeping during the day after a long mid shift, and the little ones' naps. The children's windows had bars on the outside part way up so they couldn't fall out. The walls throughout were a sunny mellow yellow-tan. The main bathroom was tiled in light blue. The tub! Oh, the tub was deep enough to really soak in! What a luxury! And the kids had such fun in it.

Fortunately, there was an elevator, although not always reliable, especially on grocery days! In the basement was a good sized laundry room with seven washers and seven dryers. There was a schedule that often wasn't kept, but rarely did we have to wait for someone else's laundry to be done.

The children loved that apartment! They'd run through the hall singing loudly to hear their echoes or pull their favorite toy, a turtle with a bell in its shell. When it warmed up enough, we'd lay a comforter on the balcony, and they'd play out there, hanging their legs through the balustrades. Not being a friend of heights, this scared me at first, but as time went on, I became accustomed to it. Regularly, we'd visit the neighbors below us to retrieve a toy that had blown onto their balcony after one of the children had tossed it over the railing. We would dispose of our Christmas tree similarly—over the railing as one of us would stand below to retrieve it. When it struck the frozen ground, all of the needles would fall off stripping the tree bare. It was a much better way than trailing dead needles through the elevator and hall. The balcony also was a landmark of sorts. Ed loves Christmas lights and would put as many as he could on the balcony. We rarely took them down before Easter, so giving directions to our place was easy—we're in the building with the lights! We tried grilling on the balcony one April, before the temperatures had come up to freezing point. The burgers never did get very hot, much less cooked.

The apartment became "party central" for much of our stay. We were on the U.S. Army shuttle and public bus routes, had a large entertainment area with a pass-thru from the kitchen that made moving food and drink very convenient. One New Year's Eve, someone, no, I won't tell who, put firecrackers in a bowl of Screaming Yellow Zonkers, candy coated popcorn & nuts. We had Zonkers dropping from the eight-foot ceilings for months. Then there was a bottle rocket exchange with some local youths, but I describe that later.

When living in military housing, there are certain standards that have to be kept, and stringent cleaning policies that need to be met at the end of your stay. Explaining how the indelible marker got on the linoleum floor seam and fridge door, and the Zonkers, yes, still some on the ceiling, got there, was interesting. Nothing was said, however, of the Snoopy Ed had painted on the balcony wall. We were told years later that it was still there!

It took some time to get the bags unpacked and finally get the children settled and into bed. I poured Edie a glass of fine German white wine, and we stepped out on the balcony. The evening was crisp and cold. As I remember, there were very few clouds, and the moon helped the street lights illuminate the neighboring buildings. A steady stream of traffic made its way up and down the street seven stories below. Through the trees, we could make out the spot lights that flooded the death strip on the other side of the ominous Wall. As with everyone who first experiences West Berlin, Edie had a million questions. She asked about the apartment, about the neighborhood, about Berlin Brigade, about my work, about the Wall, about the schools, about the Base Exchange, about the threat only yards away, about nearly everything. Her excitement was fun and infectious. I attempted to answer everything; I'm sure I fell well short of satisfying her. Our joy was shattered by burst of machine gun fire, the blare of a siren, and spot lights swinging wildly to and fro through the not-so-distant trees. Instantly, I understood what was happening so near our new home; Edie had no idea. The combined look of fear and incredulity on her face spoke volumes. Her welcome was destroyed by the reality of life adjacent to the people's paradise. It was evident that someone had tried to flee the blessings of communism and may have paid the ultimate price. I tried to explain as gently as I could what might have happened. We later found that the would-be escapee, fortunately, had not been killed. Still, I can only make an informed guess at his ultimate fate and that of anyone who had abetted his attempt.

East Germany's ex-leaders always denied they had ordered soldiers to shoot people trying to flee across the Berlin Wall, even though hundreds were killed. However, the discovery of a written order to open fire on men, women, and children served to remind all of the regime's brutality. It was always obvious that East Germany's border guards were ordered to shoot at people trying to flee to the West. Without such an order, they wouldn't have killed thousands of defectors desperately attempting to gain their freedom across the Berlin Wall or the minefields of the eight-hundred-sixty-mile border between East and West Germany. After the Berlin Wall collapsed in 1989, East Germany's former leaders and top Stasi secret service officials insisted there had been no shoot-to-kill order, and the absence of evidence to the contrary helped many of them escape prosecution or get away with lenient sentences in a series of trials.

Ironically, on the forty-sixth anniversary of the start of construction, a seven-page document surfaced in an archive of Stasi files that contains an explicit firing order. It was issued to a special team of Stasi agents tasked with infiltrating regular units of border guards, thereby denying their colleagues the option of defecting. The document was found in an archive in Magdeburg, west of Berlin, in the personnel file of a Stasi agent named only as Manfred L. who had signed the document to confirm he had read and acknowledged it. "It is your duty to use your combat...skills in such a way as to overcome the cunning of the border breacher, to challenge or liquidate him in order to thwart the planned border breach," says the order dated October 1, 1973. "Don't hesitate to use your weapon even when border breaches happen with women and children, which traitors have often exploited in the past." The order is a reminder of how ruthless the East German regime was. They were indeed vicious murderers.

Nearly five decades after the Berlin Wall was built, researchers still can't say for sure how many people were killed trying to cross it. I've read supposedly reliable estimates that range from one hundred to a staggering three hundred or more. The number wounded by weapons or injured in an attempt are impossible to calculate.

With my explanation of what just happened, Edie's joy was gone and replaced with the sobering realization that the game we occupiers played was deadly serious. Our desire to do something, anything, was frustrated as it would always be. We knew we could do nothing for the fleeing East Berliner or retaliate against those who chose to kill rather than turn a blind eye. It is a feeling one doesn't soon forget. We reentered the apartment. The children were still asleep, the apartment looked as it had twenty minutes earlier, but the atmosphere had changed and would remain so for the duration of our two tours in the city.

And so it was that Edie was introduced to Berlin, both West and East. Our two tours were remarkable, hectic, and enjoyable. We loved the city, but there was always the knowledge in the back of our minds that a life and death game was played twenty-four hours a day just yards from where we lived.

TROIKA

A general meaning of the Russian word troika (Cyrillic alphabet:) is three of a kind, a collection of three. The definition fits for the three U.S. Air Force locations that were involved in monitoring the various happenings in East Germany and elsewhere during the Cold War. I was officially assigned to TCA (Tempelhof Central Airport) while specifically assigned to Marienfelde and subsequently to Teufelsberg.

TEMPELHOF CENTRAL AIRPORT (TCA)

Air travelers to Berlin flew through one of the West Berlin air corridors. There were three regulated airways for civil and military aircraft of the Western allies. They connected Berlin with West Germany and overflew former East Germany. The airspace within these corridors was reserved for the exclusive use of U.S., British, and French-registered, noncombative aircraft belonging to the armed forces or airlines of these countries. Additionally, the planes had to be piloted by aviators holding passports of these countries.

Each of the three corridors was only twenty-five miles wide. Aircraft were compelled to fly at a maximum height of ten thousand feet. The corridors connected the three West Berlin airports of Tempelhof, Tegel, and Gatow with various West German airfields as follows:

- Northern Air Corridor: Hamburg, Bremen, Northern Europe

- Central Air Corridor: Hanover, Düsseldorf, Cologne/Bonn, Western Europe
- Southern Air Corridor: Frankfurt, Stuttgart, Munich, Nuremberg, Southern Europe

For commercial and operational reasons, all airlines routed their flights through the central corridor whenever possible as this was the shortest of the three, thereby minimizing the time the aircraft spent cruising at maximum altitude, ten thousand feet). Modern, at least for August, 1970, jet aircraft cruising at this relatively low altitude could not attain or maintain a fuel efficient cruising speed, which led to extended flight times. The central corridor provided the most economical option. It was through this corridor that my Pan Am jet traveled bringing me to Berlin for the first time.

As our plane emerged from the central corridor, I caught my first glimpse of the city. As I had been briefed, it was a modern oasis amidst a sea of obvious poverty and want. The Communist side of the divided city was bland and colorless. I remember thinking that the entire town could use a coat of paint. I would recall that assessment decades later while traveling through towns in Northern Russia as a Christian missionary. As the foreboding wall passed below us with ever present guard towers and no man's land clearly visible, the city took on a color and life that was as stark in its difference to the East as Capitalism is to Communism. As we dropped between buildings on our approach to Berlin Tempelhof Airport (German: Flughafen Berlin-Tempelhof situated in the south-central borough of Tempelhof-Schöneberg), I began to question the judgment if not the ability of our crew. With one final, abrupt drop, the plane shuddered as our wheels made contact with the approaching runway, immediately we reversed thrust. I concluded that landing at TCA was not for the faint of heart. The yawning overhang of the terminal beggared description. Frankly, it was the largest building I'd ever seen. It literally swallowed our jet and dwarfed the vehicles that approached to retrieve our luggage. It was but my first of many surprises this incredible city would provide for the next eleven years.

This enormous building hosted our headquarters, the 7350th Air Base Group (later, 7350th Support Group), and the 1946th Airborne Air Control Squadron (1948–1992). The 1946th operated the control tower and conducted operations for the then U.S. Air Force Security Service monitoring unique radar signals emanating from the other side. Located behind the Iron Curtain and operating in the middle of the combined East German and Soviet Air Forces, TCA was the perfect location to conduct Radar Intelligence (RADINT) operations. Our operation intercepted, displayed, and interpreted the radar of various East German and Russian radar controllers.

As impressive as the building was, its history was more so. Originally, the land was occupied by the Knights Templar (from whence Tempelhof got its name). The site was used as a parade field from 1720 to the beginning of World War I. Although Orville Wright piloted a demonstration flight there in 1909, it would not be officially designated as an airport until October 8, 1923. At that time, the Weimar Republic commissioned Paul and Klaus Enger to build a modern terminal. Three years later, Lufthansa was founded at the field. Designed for expansion, the new terminal was demolished after only ten years. It may have suited Weimar, but it was insufficiently grand for Adolf Hitler and the Third Reich.

Although Albert Speer would seem to have been the first choice as architect for the new structure, Hitler chose Ernst Sagebiel. Sagebiel served as office manager for one of Europe's pioneering modernists, the German Jewish architect, Erich Mendelsohn. Based in Berlin until birth of the Third Reich, Mendelsohn couldn't ignore the rising anti-Semitic policy of the government. He fled to England in 1933. Later, the Nazis seized his fortune, struck his name from the list of the German Architects' Union, and finally excluded him from the Prussian Academy of Arts. In 1914, it was he who designed a huge, quarter-mile long building he call an aerodrome. In his design, he planned a curved structure with a tall central hall to accommodate six airships and low hangars for aeroplanes.

Although Sagebiel's new masters insisted he adopt a more classic, austere design, Tempelhof is still Mendelsohn's 1914 aerodrome design in disguise. The tall central hall would accommodate people rather than airships. The curving wings with their configuration of hangars and workshops are there. Its proportions are different, and the style is wholly different, but Sagebiel had learned well from Mendelsohn.

It was one of the world's great airports. Passengers arrived at the front, traversed the Departure Hall, and walked out the back to their planes, which were drawn up under a huge canopy. Nothing could be more direct. The bulk of the complex's office space formed an expansive grand approach. The hangars curve a very long way round on either side, embracing an oval airfield. All this went on, while the main activity—arrival, process, departure—was kept within a tight central choreography. Then the largest building in Europe and third largest in the world, it incorporated a giant gallery with room for nine hundred thousand spectators. Its airside frontage runs in a continuous concave curve of three thousand eight hundred and seventy feet, or nearly three quarters of a mile. Its canopy is forty feet high, and cantilevers out one hundred and seventy feet along its entire distance. The stone eagles on the facade are finely detailed. Its elegant semi-circular structure is said to be the only man-made structure other than China's Great Wall visible from space. It was designed to last until the year 2000. It did that and more.

Its importance transcended that of an airport. The Führer saw the building as the conclusion of Speer's grandiose, and never built, north-south axis. In 1934, Hitler defended its incredible size necessary for national prestige for it was to be the "Gateway to Europe." The noted British architect, Lord Norman foster declared it "the mother of all airports." As late as 1939, expert commentators in America viewed Tempelhof as nothing more than a vehicle to facilitate the anticipated explosion in civil air travel. As a final irony, occupying American forces repaired and largely completed Sagebiel's design.

During World War II, its buildings were used to build and assemble the Junkers Ju87 "Stuka" dive bomber and the Focke Wulf FW190 fighter. On April 24, 1945, Soviet forces overran the airport. At war's end, much of Berlin was nothing but rubble. Over six hundred thousand apartments had been destroyed, and only 2.8 million of the city's original population of 4.3 million still lived there, if hand-to-mouth existence can indeed be called living. By allied agreement, the city was divided into four sectors and administered jointly by the occupying powers, the United States of America, Great Britain, France, and the Soviet Union. After this quadripartite agreement and sectoring of the city, Tempelhof was handed over to U.S. Forces on July 4th.

American Overseas Airlines started the first commercial postwar air service with a flight from New York on May 18, 1946. On May 20, 1950, U.S. Forces held the first Armed Forces Day and parade open to the public.

Of course, Tempelhof is best known as the base of the Berlin Airlift, during which an Allied aircraft landed every ninety seconds keeping the city supplied with provisions throughout the Soviet blockade of 1948-49. Such a flotilla of planes constituted a sort of aerial bridge or Luftbrücke between the West and Berlin. A three-pronged monument bearing that name and representing U.S. and British airmen killed during the Airlift was erected near the airport's entrance in 1951.

Immediately after WWII, the airport was occupied by U.S. troops. The 6912th Mobile Radio Squadron (later 6912th Electronic Security Group) of the U.S. Air Force Security Service

(USAFSS) occupied the upper floors of one of the wings. Several antennae were placed on the roof ostensibly for air traffic control. In 1984, the USAF constructed a seventy-two-meter radar tower to monitor air space. Its radar is capable of tracking aircraft at a distance of 350 km and an altitude of 30 km. The tower was turned over to the Bundeswehr in 1994.

In 1991, offices previously used by the allies were occupied by civilian airport authorities and elements of the Berlin police. Since then, various companies have rented space there.

It was here that our headquarters was located along with all of our support staff. It also housed a sophisticated radar intelligence (RADINT) operation. In fact, everything found on a normal air force base could be found at Tempelhof. While I worked at the other two air force locations during my career in Berlin, we would spend a great deal of time at Tempelhof.

To the great chagrin of all who therein served, the airport ceased operating in 2008 in the process that ultimately utilized Schönefeld as the sole commercial airport for Berlin.

MARIENFELDE

The Marienfelde compound, operated by the U.S. Air Force, was located at the southern border of the city on Diedersdorfer Weg. Marienfelde is a subdistrict of the Tempelhof district. Like our other operational location, Teufelsberg, the operational buildings were constructed on a hill made entirely of the rubble caused by allied bombing during World War II. It was my first Berlin assignment. I had served fifteen months in Wakkanai, Japan as a Russian linguist/intercept operator. I was assigned to Japan after nine months of Basic Russian language training at the U.S. Air Force Skytop compound on the campus of Syracuse University. It was one of several department of defense language schools located on college campuses throughout the United States.

Early in the 1970s, all language training was consolidated at the Defense Language Institute West Coast (DLIWC) in Monterey, California. I would attend DLIWC in 1974 for my third nine-month course, Advanced Russian Language Training. We were blessed in that virtually all of our language instructors were defectors from Stalin's horrific regime or the unrest that occurred in the years after his death. We learned communism from those who suffered the most under its benevolence. I learned to hate Stalin, his predecessors, and his descendants. In many ways, he made Hitler look humane.

Between 1962 and 1965, the United States Air Force Security Service (later the Electronic Security Command) built this intercept site for the National Security Agency. The compound included sixteen buildings, six of them "operations." They occupied an area of approximately thirteen acres. One of these structures contained the burn room where classified documents were routinely incinerated.

Ostensibly providing air traffic control, the station was used by the 6912th Electronic Security Group (690th Electronic Security Wing) for signals intelligence (SIGINT). The station performed a twenty-four-hour work schedule in four flights or work groups. The official mission was tracking allied aviation and sensing atmospheric phenomena. The Stasi claimed evidence that the site conducted electronic warfare operations, but this was never substantiated and I never observed it. The British Royal Air Force was a guest tenant.

I spent three years manning a rack of intercept equipment, intercepting, transcribing, and analyzing communications of the Soviet Air Force and working shift, our seventeen-day week. After a few shifts, it was difficult to remember just what month it was. I worked here from December 1970 thru June 1974.

In 1991, all equipment was removed and the buildings were torn down in 1992. Today, the hill is part of a recreational area. The local area boasts a number of important industries, including a Daimler Chrysler assembly plant. The main north-south rail line entering Berlin also passes through Marienfelde.

Ironically, the district of Marienfelde was also known for a large refugee processing center which operated during the Cold War. The center, which opened in 1953, was the first stop for more than 1.5 million refugees fleeing communism in East Germany via West Berlin. Refugees arriving in West Berlin were sent to the center where they received medical treatment, food, identification papers, and housing until they could be permanently resettled in the West.

Even after the fall of the Berlin Wall in 1989, the center continued processing East German refugees until unification a year later. Today, the center remains in use, processing ethnic Germans who are immigrating to Germany from the former Soviet Union.

TEUFELSBERG

Teufelsberg (German for devil's mountain) is a hill in the former West Berlin named after the nearby Teufelsee. It rises about 115 meters above the surrounding Brandenburg plain, more precisely due north of Berlin's Grunewald forest.

As stated earlier, the hill has a curious history having been built by the Allies after the Second World War from Berlin rubble during the twenty years it took to rebuild the city. One estimate for the amount of debris is approximately twelve million cubic meters, or about four hundred thousand buildings. It is higher than the highest natural hill (the Kreuzberg) in the Berlin area.

Teufelsberg's origin does not in itself make it unique, as there are many similar man-made rubble mounds in Germany (see also Marienfelde) and other war-torn cities of Europe. It's what's buried beneath that makes it special. Designed by Albert Speer, a Nazi "Wehrtechnische Institut" or military-technical college rests at the bottom of the mound. During the war, the Institut was used by the Wehrmacht to store ammunition and explosives. The Allies tried to demolish the structure with explosives, but they found that covering it with debris was easier than trying to blow it up. In the 1960s, a small skiing center was built on the slopes of the hill.

The U.S. National Security Agency (NSA) built one of its largest listening stations on top of the hill as part of the global ECHELON Signals Intelligence (SIGINT) gathering network. The hill was located in the British sector and operated jointly with the U.S. Army and Air Force. Mobile Allied listening units would drive to different locales in West Berlin hoping to gain the best vantage point for listening to Soviet and East German military traffic. One such unit drove to the top of Teufelsberg and discovered a marked improvement in listening ability. This discovery eventually led to a large structure being built atop the hill. At the request of U.S. government, the ski lifts were removed because they allegedly disturbed the optimum signal reception. The station, which concentrated on Soviet, East German, and Eastern Bloc ground operations, continued SIGINT collection until the Wall and East Germany fell. After that the station was closed and the equipment removed. The buildings and radar domes still remained in place for some time.

I worked there from 1978 to 1981 and then was assigned to a Reconnaissance unit at Strategic Air Command Headquarters, Offut AFB, Omaha, Nebraska.

All was not always professional or pro forma; some rather curious and even humorous happenstances interrupted daily operations. For instance, in the late 60s, operators noticed that signal reception significantly increased each year around the time of Volksfest, the annual German-American festival held during the summer for two weeks on the Hüttenweg in Zehlendorf at Truman Plaza about five kilometers southeast of the station. After much investigation, the 'culprit' was found. It seems the metal Ferris wheel amplified effective signal reception in a wide arc around the city. After the discovery, orders were issued and the structure remained standing for some time after the festival closed its gates.

The site and its resident units twice won the prestigious Travis Trophy. The Travis Trophy is a Department of Defense level award and the highest award any intelligence unit can win. It is awarded annually to the organization, unit or site whose activities contributed most to a specific national policy or security interest.

In the 1990s, as Berlin experienced an economic boom after reunification, a group of investors bought the hill from the City of Berlin and began to build hotels and apartments at the top. There was talk of preserving the listening station as a sort of spy museum. Berlin's building boom produced a glut of buildings, however, and the Teufelsberg project became unprofitable. The construction project was subsequently aborted. As of the early 2000s, there has been talk of the city buying back the hill. However, this is unlikely, as the area is encumbered with a mortgage of nearly fifty million dollars. Unfortunately, the site has been vandalized heavily since the company abandoned the project.

A PAIR OF SHORTS AND A LONG

Living in a city such as West Berlin was something rare indeed. The city was located 113 miles behind the Iron Curtain and had an ethereal, almost eerie mystique. After the wall went up, fully twenty-five percent of the population was involved in espionage or intelligence gathering for one of several powers, both East and West. Crime was nearly nonexistent due to the dual facts that the espionage element was reluctant to draw attention themselves, and the West Berlin Police Force rivaled the military of many countries. That being said, the majority of its inhabitants were decidedly fatalistic. The Soviets and East Germans had a history of "saber rattling," and threatening the city. The atmosphere had an impact on one's psyche and behavior. The following stories represent those that have some veracity attached to them, either through the sheer number of people who told them or through personal witness.

SHORT 1: BATTLING BRITS

This is one of those tales that I cannot verify. It may or may not have occurred prior to our arrival in West Berlin. If it isn't true, it should be. Regardless, the story does demonstrate the mindset of those who worked within Berlin's confines surrounded by an enemy that was at best unpredictable.

One evening, I found myself sharing pints with members of the British Rugby Club. At least I think that was the name. The club was the pride and joy of those who played the venerable and deadly game of rugby. As I learned that evening, in the United

Kingdom, an old saying states that "football (soccer) is a gentleman's game played by thugs, and rugby is a game for thugs played by gentlemen." Whatever the case, the sport is not for the timid.

While reveling with my hosts and viewing their memorabilia, one of their number began to share a story that was said to have occurred sometime around the middle 1960s at RAF Gatow.

The British 26th Signals Regiment operated a small listening post at RAF Gatow Airport in the Spandau District of West Berlin. The closest military neighbor to RAF Gatow was a tank unit of the National People's Army of East Germany. This was located immediately opposite the airfield, behind the section of the Berlin Wall that ran along the western side of the airfield, and was clearly visible from RAF Gatow's control tower. The Berlin Wall section opposite Gatow was not in fact a wall, but a wire fence. East Germany claimed that this was a "military courtesy," but nobody at RAF Gatow believed this, thinking that it was instead intended to make a military invasion easier. This surmise was confirmed after the reunification of Germany, when the East German invasion plans for West Berlin, codenamed "Operation Centre" were found. The invasion plans were continually updated, even in 1990 when it was clear that East Germany would soon cease to exist.

RAF Gatow would later gain notoriety when an East German defector chose to land his plane there. D-EWOH is a Zlin Z42M General Aviation aircraft. Prior to the registration of its current tail number in 1991, it was registered in the German Democratic Republic as DDR–WHO. It was stolen from the Gesellschaft für Sport und Technik (a German military youth organization) on 15 July 1987 and flown from Schoenhagen in East Germany to RAF Gatow (now General-Steinhoff Kaserne) in West Berlin by Thomas Kruger in order to facilitate his defection to the Allies from Soviet controlled East Berlin.

It was later returned by road, passing through the Berlin Wall, although members of the RAF had adorned it with slogans like, "Wish you were here," "Come back soon!"

With such precarious proximity to the Wall, the tank unit, and a guard tower observing daily operations, the Brits were eager to show the commies that they were a force to be dealt with. Military protocol called for a morning formation and roll call. Each morning, according to my source at the club, the next shift of Signals Corps troops would dutifully "fall in" and "sound off." This went on daily under the penetrating stare of East German tower guards and their ever present field glasses. That is, it went on until one fateful autumn morning.

The troops formed as usual, gave their pro forma report, and were ready to be dismissed and begin work when three daring souls seeking infamy broke ranks before being dismissed. This act would not normally cause much more than a good "chewing out" from the sergeant major, but it's what they did next that caused such a stir. One dashed directly at the ersatz wall carrying a length of stovepipe. When he was within a few paces of the fence, he jammed the pipe into the ground with the top end aimed directly at the tower. Closely following, both colleagues arrived at the stovepipe and performed their duties flawlessly. The second grabbed the pipe as if to steady and assure its aim while the third produced a blackened coffee can, which he slammed down the pipe with force. That done, the first and third cupped their hands over their ears while spinning away from the tower.

Meanwhile, the East German guards grew more and more anxious. Unsure what the three madmen were doing, they must have fingered their weapons more than once. Seeing what they must have thought was a mortar being fired at their position, they had only a split second to settle on their next action. Both guards came to the same conclusion simultaneously and without hesitation dove out adjacent open windows. The twenty to thirty foot fall apparently caused some formidable injuries because the guards moaned and barely moved until retrieved by their comrades. Meanwhile, the sergeant major managed to corral the three, dismissed the rest, and got everyone safely inside.

The actions of the three constituted an international incident with all the diplomatic wrangling that normally ensued. To avoid the threat of additional reprisal, the British decided that the perpetrators could better serve Her Majesty elsewhere in the Empire. With typical speed and dispatch, the men were on a plane out of West Berlin that evening thereby making mute some of the East German vitriol that followed.

I asked what happened to the Brits and the East Germans. The storyteller was evasive concerning the Brits and had no clue what happened to the Germans. When I questioned him about the timetable for the event, he was equally evasive giving rise to no small amount of skepticism on my part. I still remain skeptical, even though I heard the same tale from several others during my near decade in the city. True or not, those of us who despised the East German guards and loved the Brits choose to believe the story.

SHORT 2: FLYING FIRST SERGEANT

Although this tale was supported by testimony from several witnesses, its plausibility is still more than somewhat suspect. I relate it because the names, dates, and units revealed to me actually existed at the time. Regardless, the story was told more than once, and given the time and nature of soldiers and airmen who served then, I suppose it is not beyond the realm of possibility.

In the U.S. Army, the rank of first sergeant is above the rank of sergeant first class, below the rank of sergeant major, and shares the pay grade of E-8 with master sergeants; the rank is abbreviated as 1SG. Master sergeants are laterally promoted to first sergeant upon selection by the senior leadership at Battalion or higher depending on the location of the company in the Army Organizational Table. Upon reassignment to a non first sergeant billet, the soldier reverts back to their original rank of master sergeant. First sergeants are generally the senior noncommissioned officers of company (battery, troop) sized units and are commonly referred to as "top," "top kick," or "top hat," due to their seniority and their position at the top of the company's enlisted ranks. They are also sometimes referred to as "second hat," in recognition that even though a company includes several lieutenants, it is more often the first sergeant that the company commander will turn to when entrusting important responsibilities. Often, the company commander will hold the 1SG accountable for the morale and behavior of the enlisted force within his/her command.

Such was the case of one of the company's in Berlin Brigade. The name of the unit will remain anonymous as will the name of the first sergeant. According to all reports, the man was an ogre. It was said that ultimate power corrupts ultimately, well assumed or wished-for power has a worse impact. Apparently, the company commander relied over much on the first sergeant to the point of abrogation of command duties. The 1SG enjoyed carte blanche when it came to the enlisted force. A better man would have turned the company into a dedicated military unit, ready to take on any task with confidence and competence. This man, however, allowed a bit of power to swell an already inflated ego. He lorded his position over every one under his command. That coupled with a temper that was characterized by extremes, and the rank and file developed a deep and abiding hate for the man.

Men and women already under daily duress will find a way of minimizing or eliminating any additional pressure. After nearly a year of cow towing to the first sergeant's increasingly ridiculous demands, some of the more creative and enterprising sergeants in the company came up with a plan to rid themselves of this man. Fragging had gone out with the end of the Vietnam War, plus the practice carried with it the real threat of execution. Something short of death but sufficient to get rid of him had to happen. The final decision made was to take the man to town for his upcoming birthday. That may not sound like a form of retribution, but the result was exactly what the company envisioned.

Unknown to the commander, the sergeants invited the first sergeant for a night on the town to celebrate his birthday. Only an egomaniac would be blind to the fact that everyone in the unit hated his shadow. He must have thought that he had finally been accepted. That would prove to be a huge mistake. Careful not to go to any of their normal watering holes, they traveled into the center of the city and went to places unknown to the 1SG. The reason for this was simple; none of the sergeants wanted to be seen by anyone who could later incriminate them. The night progressed as might be expected with everyone but the guest of honor buying round after round of Schutheiss, Becks, or Berliner Kindl. Without much coaxing, the first sergeant began to display behavior he would have disciplined strongly had it been displayed by anyone else in the company. Before long, he was roaring drunk.

The first sergeant's inebriated condition was the signal that the cabal had awaited. They summoned a taxi and made for the infamous Checkpoint Charlie. Actually, they went to a street about two blocks from the East-West portal. On their way, the first sergeant lapsed into a semi-coherent stupor, much the better for the plan about to be hatched. With the help of his hosts, the man staggered, or was drug, to the Berlin Wall. With more acrimony than ceremony, they hoisted the birthday boy atop the wall and with little regard for the mines or dogs that were present in several sectors; let him drop into East Berlin! They then made a hasty retreat back to their barracks and, to my knowledge, have kept mum about the incident to date.

East German Volkspolizei (VOPO's) had no training in preventing someone jumping the wall from West to East. It simply never happened; well, almost never. They must have been more than a little surprised. Their naturally suspicious nature and fear of making a scene no doubt caused them to act quietly, alerting no one at the checkpoint to the incident. Apparently, they collected their inebriated defector and took him directly to the nearest Stasi headquarters. The first sergeant awoke with a massive hangover in a stark, sparsely decorated, cold, damp room. He was sitting in a wooden chair, and in front of him was a decrepit wooden table. On the other side of the table was an East German officer shouting something incoherent. His face was partially obscured by a shadow cast from the single overhead bulb dangling from a frayed wire. The American's first thought was, *Where the %$#& am I? And who is this sumbitch screaming at me?* It didn't take long to figure out what was happening, and once reality set in so did fear and an overwhelming feeling of being powerless to make it go away. Apparently, our hero spent no less than ten days as a guest of the East German Stasi/Police enduring round after endless round of interrogations. He couldn't tell them anything because there was nothing to tell. Evidently, the East Germans grew weary of the sot and decided to return him. After some hasty negotiation, he was returned through Checkpoint Charlie mere yards from the spot where his adventure began. According to the report I heard, he returned a changed man.

LONG: ONE IF BY LAND

During the 1970s–80s, the American Yacht Club in Berlin was located in the basement of the villa at Am Sandwerder 17 almost directly across from the villa where the Wannsee Conference that sealed the fate of some six million Jews was held. Today, that building is a museum.

The club was a social organization as well as a place where GIs and their dependents could learn the rudiments of sailing and advance as far as they wished in the sport. My family and I spent many hours sailing and socializing at the club. Some of our closest friends and competitors were the members of allied yacht clubs in the city. The Brits and the French had wonderful organizations. They regularly sailed rings around us in regattas. When we won one, it was cause for lengthy and robust celebration.

Although relations with each club were cordial, we seemed to have much more in common with the Brits. That and the fact that they were nearer meant we spent more time with them than with the French. As friends and occasional competitors, we naturally pulled each other's chain just for fun. One such instance is the topic of this chapter.

In the late 70s, I found myself vice commodore of the club for a couple of years. I spent considerable time bolstering our good relations with both the Brits and the French. As midsummer approached in 1979, the British Club decided to put our good relationship to the test. They loved sport and enjoyed nothing more than putting one over on the "colonials" as they were fond of calling us. Late in the evening of July 3rd, a small but well-trained group from their club sneaked onto our property and confiscated our burgee. The date of the theft was not coincidence.

The next morning, before we would have made our way to the club to engage in patriotic festivities celebrating the fourth, I received a call informing me of the previous evening's deed. I immediately comprehended the gravity of the attack. Our honor had been impinged; the gauntlet had been tossed. We had little choice but to retaliate. We would retrieve our burgee and restore our reputation.

After several hasty calls to the commodore and other members of our circle, my family and I hastened to the club. For the next two hours we made plans, gathered materials, consumed suitable libation, and levied assignments.

The plan upon which we finally agreed included sending a party by sea to attack the British Yacht Club in force with the prime objective of landing, scaling the yardarm, and retrieving our burgee. To this effort, we dedicated some fifteen to twenty sloops. Our noncombatants would follow those tasked with engaging the enemy. The secondary objective of this force was to draw attention away from an attack from the rear.

For better or worse, the club selected me to lead this rear action. The plan was for seven of us to dress as Native Americans, reminiscent of the Boston Tea Party, and to attack when we heard the melee at their dock.

A little after noon, the majority of the club set sail while the seven rangers drove to the British Yacht Club. Apparently, the sail was uneventful and everyone enjoyed the short trip. About one-half league away from the British Club, a couple of sharp-eyed Brits spotted our craft. We knew they would be prepared but had no idea just how much preparation had been accomplished. We would soon find out.

While our boats were nearing shore, the seven of us parked our vehicle at the beginning of the drive that led to the club. We would move quietly on foot for the rest of the trip. Apparently, as we were sneaking down the quiet road our boats were entering the small cove created by a small spit of land on one side and their long dock on the other. To slow the approach of our boats, they had acquired simulated incendiary grenades from their armory. They would not ignite or fragment, but they would explode with one heck of blast. If they went off in close proximity to your body, injury would result. For a couple of minutes, our boat crews weren't sure what to do. But, after they'd seen a couple of the things explode, they decided to proceed with all haste.

With the Brits occupied, we decided to make our move. It was at this moment that a van came into view speeding down the long drive. When the vehicle came alongside our band, it screeched to a halt. It was then that we noticed the logo painted on the side, BBC. A reporter jumped out of the vehicle with microphone in hand. She explained that the British Club had called earlier that morning saying that the colonials would attack the club later that day. She proceeded to ask if we were the force they had been told about. When we replied that the main force could be heard merely 150 yards away already engaged with the Brits, she gave us a curious glance, hopped back into the van, and ordered the driver to drive on. That's when we stepped in front of the van. We instructed the driver to shut the vehicle down. At first he disagreed, but wielding our fake tomahawks, we were able to persuade him to comply. We escorted the driver, reporter and cameraman to a ditch alongside the road and assigned two of our number to keep them there. When they asked what was happening, I informed them that they were prisoners of war. After all, they were British and we couldn't trust them to keep our presence secret. Thankfully, in the spirit of the event and to avoid a messy international incident, they complied when we promised to free them as soon as we were discovered.

With the current enemy safely in custody, the remainder of our small band pressed on toward the melee at the club. When we reached the gate, the sight we beheld was exhilarating. Our club had made shore and with only one of our craft capsized in the shallow water. Americans and Brits were entangled in what looked to be several scrums around the grounds. It was while everyone was otherwise engaged that we attacked. Actually, we ran as quickly as possible to the yardarm ready to shinny up the pole and retrieve our burgee. When the first of our number hit the yardarm, he found the pole covered with grease. We heard laughter at our rear; it was the BBC gleefully recording the event. The Brits had done a masterful job of greasing the yardarm over its entire length. It was impressive and frustrating.

While I was contemplating the task at hand, the Brits decided to reenact the Boston Tea Party in reverse. Rather than watching American patriots dump tea into Boston Harbor, they decided to dump colonials dressed in Indian garb into their bay. With a shout, they gathered us up en masse and chucked us in. We clamored ashore leaving dripping war paint and soggy feathers in our wake.

Eventually, the scrums disbanded as the Brits backed off, drew a few pints, and began to roar with laughter as our more energetic crew members attempted to reach the purloined burgee. After several attempts, they managed to construct a human pyramid of sorts. At long last, our flag was once again in our custody. As the last American reached the ground, I noticed a strange blue tinge beneath the gobs of grease on each person who had scaled the pole. When I asked the British commodore about the origin of the strange coloration, he could barely contain himself. "Well, mate," he replied, "it seems we neglected to warn you about the indelible blue dye we painted on before we greased the pole." And, they had. Once the grease was wiped off, a rich, royal blue dye appeared on the skin of each person who attempted or actually climbed the pole. Those who made it to the top and slid down its length sported a blue streak from the right or left side of their faces to the bottom of whatever exposed piece of skin made contact. Months later, it was not unusual to pass a still embarrassed soldier or airman with an all too visible blue streak clashing with their uniform.

With the battle over and a truce declared, both clubs resumed cordial relations. Our guests opened their well-stocked bar while others began to prepare lunch. We were told that we were in for a new-taste experience. After a moderate wait measured in the number of pints consumed, our hosts gleefully served up mushy peas and bangers. For sailors used to the taste of burgers and fries, this was a considerable stretch. Frankly, we had never seen food look quite like that. However, with the help of Guinness, we managed to consume the feast and settle in to a very pleasant end to a rather exciting day. We were even able to relive our exploits on the evening news via the BBC. One comment caught my attention, "Repeat of the Revolutionary War," indeed.

WE CALLED HIM PRINCE JIM

It was during our second full year in Berlin that we met the irrepressible Jim. If memory serves, he was a technical sergeant, but his demeanor and behavior left one with the impressions that he was related to European royalty. He took a distinct liking to my family and doted on our children. He was forever bringing small but expensive gifts of food, wine, and incredible confections. He was kind, humorous, well manned, articulate, and a great storyteller over a wide range of topics. We all liked him and thoroughly enjoyed sharing quiet, cultured evenings with him.

In our naiveté, we never questioned where Jim acquired such treats or even how he could afford his sophisticated taste on a tech sergeant's pay. Looking back, we no doubt ignored the obvious out of friendship and fear of discovering something unsavory about our friend.

As our relationship grew, Jim began to confide more and more in us about his extracurricular activities. He was an accomplished photographer, and he said that he earned extra money doing family photographs; however, he never offered to take ours. Further, according to Jim, he was well acquainted with more than one vintner in West Germany and even had his own special German white wine bearing his personal label. He said that he was rewarded handsomely for his ability to market the wine in Berlin. He gave us more than one bottle of his special reserve. It was exquisite. As time went on, he told us tales of other ventures that he and other well healed entrepreneurs had undertaken. Although some of his endeavors were shrouded in secrecy, we saw Jim merely as an ambitious type-A, who enjoyed the quiet and calm of a family once in a while.

I remember being summoned to the first sergeant's office. Upon arrival, the first shirt began to interrogate me about our relationship with Jim. I was a bit shaken by the line of questioning and my interrogator made good use of it. Fortunately for me and my family, I was only able to relate Jim's kindness towards us and how much we cared for him. That's when the sergeant told me that Jim had been arrested by the OSI.

Bewildered and upset by the revelation, I begged for more information. What I learned still seems more fantasy than fact. It seems that the OSI had been watching Jim for some time. They had suspected him of partaking in various activities that were not only criminal, but could be used to blackmail him into revealing classified information. His final act was to negotiate the sale of an automatic machine gun to an undercover agent. Apparently, the sale took some time to develop, but when Jim produced the weapon, the agent produced his badge and handcuffs. I was in shock, but what happened next truly threw me for a loop. The first shirt then informed me that Jim had named me executor of his estate while he was incarcerated. I was handed the keys to Jim's apartment and ordered to inventory everything in it. With that, the sergeant dismissed me with a comment about choosing better friends. I didn't reply, but I wanted to say something about the United States trusting this man with a top secret cryptographic clearance. I suppose I should have been more discerning than our government.

When I got home and explained everything that happened, the response of my young family was unanimous—Jim was innocent! He could not have done something so stupid! He could not have that much hubris and blatant disregard for the law. How could anyone try to see automatic weapons in occupied West Berlin, 113 miles behind the Iron Curtain, within yards of the wall, in the middle of the Cold War? No, there must be some mistake.

It was only after the news broke within the squadron did I begin to hear tales of Jim's activities. It seems many of the stories he told us over a glass of wine after a fine dinner at our house were true, but they hadn't gone far enough. Natural embellishment aside, our dear friend was something of an international culprit involved in more than one activity that could earn him a lengthy stay in Manheim stockade or even worse, Fort Leavenworth, Kansas.

Again, the location and time made his actions more nefarious than they might have been in a less visible and notorious place. West Berlin was swarming with intelligence operatives in the early 1970s. Any criminal activity was immediately noticed by friend and foe alike. I believe Jim thought himself too crafty, too smooth to be caught. He was anything but an idiot. Selling guns to persons unknown was ignorant in the extreme. Even if the buyers identified themselves, there was no way for Jim to know their true identity. He was too smart to use our intelligence sources to assist in his crimes. At least, I think he was too smart. I'll never know.

The day after the first sergeant dropped the bombshell, I went to the prince's apartment. There was little doubt that the OSI had searched the apartment for evidence that would support their case; however, once I received the keys they were denied further entry. There was no doubt that Jim's arrest was a coup for the OSI and other investigative services (CID, etc.) that might have been involved. I'm sure they wanted another look. Everything appeared to be in place. If it wasn't, I would have known because Jim had given a meticulously detailed description of its contents and their exact location. I was followed, but that was normal for the city. Once inside, I was more than aware that my inventory would be scrutinized by more than the first sergeant and the court martial that was being convened.

As I began the process of inventory and discovery, I became aware of Jim's wide variety of interests. He had the best cameras I'd ever seen. My wife worked at the camera counter at the post exchange. Jim's equipment far outshone those sold there. I even found a Hasselblad among the others. That, however, was not what captured my attention. He had hundreds of pictures of local German and air force personnel. To my surprise, many of them depicted female members of our squadron in varying degrees of undress. If the pictures were released, those pictured would lose their clearances at the very least. The discovery presented me with a dilemma. How would I list this photo inventory? If I entered them merely as various photos, was I being truthful? If, however, I gave a detailed description of the cache, I ran the very real risk of ruining more than one career.

While wrestling with my decision, the first sergeant called. It seems that Jim's phone had not been disconnected. I made a mental note to do just that the next day. The reason for his call was simple. Jim had requested a nail file that resided in the top drawer of his dresser. The procedure for such a request went something like this: first, Jim had to make the request to the Military Police (MPs) at the brig, then the MPs would call Jim's first sergeant indicating exactly where the requested item was and what it looked like, the first sergeant then contacted the executor to set up a meeting at the apartment, the executor would release the item to the first sergeant who would sign for it, the executor would attach the signed document to the official inventory, and the first sergeant would immediately bring the item to the brig to turn over to the MPs. It was a tedious process but one that was necessary given the people with whom the MPs dealt.

The shirt showed up within an hour of his call. He described the item as a small black box that would be found in the right front corner of the top drawer of the dresser. I found and retrieved the nail set, turned it over, witnessed the signature, and bid farewell to my visitor. I thought nothing of the transaction. I was still reeling over my earlier discovery and was thankful that I hadn't left any pictures out for other eyes to see. It took a couple of hours for me to complete the first pass. I would be more meticulous the next day. I went home.

The next day, the buzz at the site where I worked was incredible. Everyone was joking about the events of the past evening. Unaware, I approached my best friend and asked what happened. Speaking through a broad grin, he told me the incredible tale. It seems that Jim still harbored a grudge against our first sergeant. The grudge was satisfied with him asking that his nail kit be delivered to the jail. What no one but Jim knew was that the black monogrammed box contained not a manicure kit but a lock pick set! Unfortunately, the MPs didn't share Jim's sense of humor for they jacked the first sergeant against the wall and searched him. After that, they questioned him for the better part of an hour. I was not as amused as my friend as I knew the sergeant would believe that I must have known what was in the box.

To my surprise, the recipient of Jim's wrath let it go. He didn't laugh it off as much as he just seemed to forget the entire incident. I was more than thankful. My next call came from both the attorney for the defense and the attorney for the prosecution. Each wanted me to testify. I ended up testifying for the defense. Even though Jim had committed a crime, I was there merely to relate what he had done for my family and me. I hadn't been a witness or accomplice in any of his activities, and though we had apparently benefitted from his larceny, we had not been aware of where Jim got our gifts.

Jim received twenty-five years at Fort Leavenworth, Kansas. I thought the sentence excessive, but I had no say in the matter. The last time I saw my friend was in the court room. I've had no contact with him since that last encounter. I do wonder what happened to him and pray that he made it through those years behind bars.

Oh, and all those photos, etc.? I must have received twenty phone calls from ladies in our unit begging me to turn over certain pictures they knew existed. Of course, I could not. My duties were clear, and I had investigators watching my every move. I assured each that none other than Jim would ever see them. After some deliberation, I opted to list the stash as miscellaneous photographs. After seeing Jim sentenced, I couldn't bear to put others through the same travail I had witnessed. I was far from a saint, and I reasoned that their mistake paled in comparison to Jim's.

I finally completed the inventory. I turned it in to the first sergeant and received approval to box and ship all of Jim's belongings to his official residence in the states.

Case closed.

PERSPECTIVE

The Cold War brought us to Berlin and other locations around the world. Unlike declared wars, this event spanned some forty-six years. Untold thousands on all sides died or had their lives permanently altered by the events that occurred in this west versus east conflict.

To put the book and its characters in perspective, I thought it might be appropriate to refresh the reader of certain highlights of this undeclared conflict from its inception to conclusion.

1945

- February 4–11: Yalta Conference and the initial indicators of allied mistrust that will result in the Cold War.
- May 8: VE Day–Victory in Europe. Germany surrenders to the Red Army in Berlin.
- July: Convinced the Russians already know, President Harry S. Truman informs our Soviet allies that the United States has an atomic bomb.
- August 2: The Potsdam Accord divides Europe. Misinformed and ill advised, the Western Allies allow the division of Europe and Berlin into four zones.
- August 6: United States drops the atomic bomb on Hiroshima.
- August 8: Russia enters war against Japan.
- August 9: United States drops the atomic bomb on Nagasaki.
- August 14: Japan surrenders and World War II ends.

- August 15: Emperor Hirohito announces Japan's surrender. A shocked and traumatized nation hears their emperor's voice for the first time.

1946

- February 9: In a speech designed to show hostility to the west, Stalin declares that communism and capitalism were incompatible. He further stated that capitalism was the cause of both World Wars.

- March 5: After receiving an honorary degree from Westminster College in Fulton, Missouri, Sir Winston Churchill declared, "From Stettin in the Baltic to Trieste in the Adriatic, an 'Iron Curtain' has descended across the continent." Thus, his description of the division between western powers and the area controlled by the Soviet Union marked the de facto onset of the Cold War.

1947 – DOCTRINE OF CONTAINMENT INITIATED

- March: Truman declares the U.S. will take an active role in the Greek Civil War.
- April 16: White House confidante, Bernard Baruch, coins the term Cold War.
- June 5: Secretary of State Jim Marshall develops a financial plan to rebuild Europe. The U.S. would eventually spend $12.4 billion reconstructing Europe under the plan named for him.

- September 2: Rio Pact–The U.S. and nineteen Latin American countries establish a security zone around the hemisphere.

1948

- February: Czechoslovakian coup d'état– the Communist Party of Czechoslovakia, with Soviet backing, assumed undisputed control over the government of Czechoslovakia.
- March 2: Truman's Loyalty Program created to catch Cold War spies.
- March 17: Brussels Pact organized to protect Europe from communism.
- June 24: In an attempt to force the French, United Kingdom, and United States to abandon West Berlin, Joseph Stalin seals off the city resulting in the Berlin Airlift.
- June 26: The Berlin Airlift known as "Operation Vittles" begins.

1949

- April 4: The North Atlantic Treaty Organization is founded and ratified later in the year.
- August 29: The Soviet Union tests its first atomic bomb.
- September: Communist revolutionary Mao Zedong takes control of China.
- September 30: The Berlin Airlift ends with the lifting of the Soviet blockade. It lasted 462 days. Total flights: US–189,963; UK–87,841; France–424. Miles flown:

134 million or almost 1.5 times to the sun. Deaths from crashes: US–31; British–39, at least nine Germans. Busiest twenty-four hours: April 15–16, 1949–1,398 flights, (one landing nearly every minute) off loaded 12,940 tons of cargo.
- October 1: Communist Mao Zedong establishes the People's Republic of China.
- December 1: General Chiang Kai-shek flees to Formosa and creates a Nationalist government.
- February: Senator Joseph McCarthy begins his search for Communists and Soviet spies and sympathizers inside the United States federal government and elsewhere.
- June: The Korean War begins with the United States backing the South and the People's Republic of China backing the North. The Soviet Union provides a squadron of pilots to fly the new MiG-15.

1951

- January 12: The United States Federal Civil Defense Administration is established.
- April 11: Truman fires MacArthur.

1952

- November 1: The United States detonates the first hydrogen bomb at Enewetak atoll in the Marshall Islands of the Western Pacific.

1953

- March 5: Soviet dictator Josef Stalin dies resulting in a power struggle that would culminate in Nikita Khrushchev becoming the first secretary of the Communist Party of the Soviet Union.
- March 17-June 4: Conducted at the Nevada Test Site, Operation UPSHOTKNOTHOLE consisted of 11 nuclear tests, a number exceeding that of any previous nuclear test series.
- April 15: The RAND report on the "Vulnerability of U. S. Strategic Air Power" April 15, 1953, warned of danger of Russian bomber attack because the U.S. had no warning system.
- June 19: Ethel Greenglass Rosenberg (September 28, 1915–June 19, 1953) and Julius Rosenberg (May 12, 1918–June 19, 1953), American communists, were executed for conspiracy to commit espionage. The charges related to passing information about the atomic bomb to the Soviet Union. This was the first execution of civilians for espionage in United States history.
- July 27: North and South Korea sign an armistice ending hostilities but not the war.
- August 19: Iranian coup d'état (known as the 28 Mordad coup in Iran), was the overthrow of the democratically elected government of Iranian Prime Minister Mohammad Mosaddegh. It was orchestrated by the intelligence agencies of the United Kingdom and the United States (CIA). The coup launched twenty-six years of dictatorship under Mohammad-Rezā Shāh Pahlavi, who relied heavily on U.S. support to hold onto power until the Shah himself was overthrown in February 1979.
- September: Khrushchev becomes first secretary of the Communist Party of the Soviet Union.

- December 8: "Atoms for Peace" was the title of a speech delivered by U.S. President Dwight D. Eisenhower to the UN General Assembly in New York City on December 8, 1953. "I feel impelled to speak today in a language that in a sense is new—one which I, who have spent so much of my life in the military profession, would have preferred never to use. That new language is the language of atomic warfare." The United States then launched an Atoms for Peace program that supplied equipment and information to schools, hospitals, and research institutions within the U.S. and throughout the world. The first nuclear reactors in Iran and Pakistan were built under the program by American machine and foundry.

1954

- January 1: The Soviet Government forms the KGB (КГБ or Комитет государственной безопасности– Komitet gosudarstvennoy bezopasnosti) or committee for state security.
- May/June: The Guatemalan coup d'état was a covert operation organized by the United States Central Intelligence Agency to overthrow Jacobo Árbenz Guzmán, the democratically-elected President of Guatemala. Árbenz's government put forth a number of new policies, such as seizing and expropriating unused, unfarmed land that private corporations set aside long ago and giving the land to peasants. The U.S. intelligence community deemed such plans communist in nature. This led CIA director Allen Dulles to fear that Guatemala would become a "Soviet beachhead in the western hemisphere."
- July: United States involvement in Vietnam began in the early 1950s. The Truman administration supported

France's colonial war against the Communist nationalists, known as the Viet Minh, in their contention for independence. The Eisenhower administration continued this support with military aid. However, France was unable to keep fighting. In 1954, the Geneva Accords were signed. The agreement split Vietnam at the 17th parallel until unified elections, which were to be held in 1956. It also forbade the presence of foreign troops in Vietnam. Since the United States refused to sign the Geneva Accords, it remained the primary supporter of anticommunist efforts in South Vietnam.

1955

- May 14: The Warsaw Treaty (1955–91) is signed. It is the informal name for the "Treaty of Friendship, Cooperation and Mutual Assistance," commonly known as the Warsaw Pact, creating the Warsaw Treaty Organization. The treaty was a mutual defense treaty subscribed to by eight communist states in Eastern Europe. It was established at the USSR's initiative.

1956

- June 29: The Soviet Union sends tanks into Poznan, Poland, to suppress worker's demonstrations.v
- July 26: Egypt seizes the Suez Canal. On 16 May, Nasser officially recognized the People's Republic of China. This angered the U.S. and its secretary of state, John Foster Dulles, a keen sponsor of Taiwan. This move, coupled with the impression that the project was beyond Egypt's

economic capabilities, caused Eisenhower to withdraw all American financial aid for the Aswan Dam project on 19 July. Nasser's response was the nationalization of the Suez Canal. On 26 July, in a speech in Alexandria, Nasser gave a riposte to Dulles. During his speech he deliberately mentioned the name of Ferdinand de Lesseps, the builder of the canal, a code-word for Egyptian forces to seize control of the canal and implement its nationalization. He announced that the Nationalization Law had been published, that all assets of the Suez Canal Company had been frozen, and that stockholders would be paid the price of their shares according to the day's closing price on the Paris Stock Exchange.

- September 4: USSR sends military aid to Afghanistan.
- November 10: The Hungarian revolt against the country's Soviet-dominated regime begins on October 23rd and ousts the government. Soviet troops invade on November 4th, starting a week of bitter fighting. When it was over, Soviet forces had imposed control. Two thousand five hundred Hungarians and seven hundred Soviet troops died in the revolt and widespread repression followed.

1957

- August 26: The USSR launches the "Vostok" (East) rocket, the world's first icbM.
- October 4: The Soviets beat the U.S. into space by launching the first human-made satellite, Sputnik 1, into orbit. The common translation of Sputnik is "traveling companion of the Earth." When the satellite was first launched, the New York Times gave the name's literal meaning as, "something that is traveling with a traveler" with the

explanation, "the traveler is the earth, traveling through space, and the companion 'traveling with' it is the satellite."

1958

- January 31: Explorer 1, the first United States earth satellite, is launched in participation with the International Geophysical Year.
- July: NASA begins the Mercury project using Atlas rockets.
- November: Khrushchev demands the allies withdraw troops from West Berlin.

1959

- February 16: Fidel Alejandro Castro Ruz sworn in as Prime Minister of Cuba.
- September: Khrushchev visits United States; engages in the "Kitchen Debate."

1960

- May 1: Flying out of Peshawar, Pakistan, U.S. pilot Francis Gary Powers is shot down in his U-2 spy plane over the Soviet Union. In a well-staged show trial, he is convicted of espionage only to be traded on February 10, 1962 in the most famous "spy swap" of the Cold War.
- September 1960: The Martin and Mitchell Defection occurred when two National Security Agency (NSA) cryptologists, William Hamilton Martin and Bernon F.

Mitchell, defected to the Soviet Union. A secret 1963 NSA study said that "Beyond any doubt, no other event has had, or is likely to have in the future, a greater impact on the agency's security program." Their unchecked access at NSA caused the intelligence community to consider and eventually institute compartmentalization.
- November: John F. Kennedy elected President of the United States.
- December 19: Cuba openly aligns itself with the Soviet Union.

1961

- April 15: Bay of Pigs invasion–a fiasco occurs when a group of CIA-backed exiles attempts to mount an invasion of communist Cuba. The U.S. abandons the exiles.
- August 13: East Germany closes its border with the West in an attempt to halt a "brain drain." Thousands of professionals had fled to the west leaving a labor shortage in the GDR that would never be entirely filled.
- August 17: Construction of Berlin Wall begins.

1962

- 1962: The U.S. increases its involvement in Viet Nam. However, on November 15, 1963 (just days before his assassination) President John F. Kennedy announces the withdrawal of one thousand advisers for December, of what was meant to be an overall reduction of U.S. Forces in Vietnam.

- October 16: Cuban missile crisis–Soviets secretly install nuclear weapons on Cuba, ninety miles from U.S. mainland. President Kennedy orders a naval blockade. As the two superpowers confront each other, the world holds its breath. It is the nearest the super powers and the world would come to a nuclear exchange. The Soviets blink first and agree to withdraw their missiles. I remember it vividly.

1963

- January 23: Senior British intelligence officer Kim Philby, who with Guy Burgess and Donald McLean made up the most famous trio of British Soviet agents, disappears and later surfaces in Moscow. There he becomes steeped in vodka, dying in 1988.
- June 20: A hotline is established between the White House and the Kremlin.
- June 26: President Kennedy makes his "Ich bin ein Berliner" speech in West Berlin.
- August 5: President Kennedy signs the Nuclear Test Ban Treaty.
- November 22: Lee Harvey Oswald assassinates President Kennedy in Dallas. No foreign intervention is ever proved, but conspiracy suspicions linger to this day.

1964

- April 20: President Lyndon Johnson and Soviet Premier Nikita Khrushchev announce plans to reduce the production of nuclear weapons material.

- August 2: Gulf of Tonkin Incident.
- October: Leonid Brezhnev deposes Nikita Khrushchev and becomes First Secretary.
- October: China develops the atomic bomb.

1965

- April: Five hundred U.S. troops invade the Dominican Republic to crush a popular revolt aimed at returning John Bosch to power. The U.S. presence in the Dominican quickly grows, with an additional four thousand troops arriving a few days later. Eventually, a force of twenty-three thousand will occupy the country.
- July 28: During a noontime press conference, President Johnson announces he will send forty-four combat battalions to Vietnam increasing the U.S. military presence to one hundred twenty-five thousand men. Monthly draft calls are doubled to thirty-five thousand. "I have asked the commanding general, General Westmoreland, what more he needs to meet this mounting aggression. He has told me. And we will meet his needs. We cannot be defeated by force of arms. We will stand in Vietnam." "...I do not find it easy to send the flower of our youth, our finest young men, into battle. I have spoken to you today of the divisions and the forces and the battalions and the units, but I know them all, every one. I have seen them in a thousand streets, of a hundred towns, in every state in this union, working and laughing and building, and filled with hope and life. I think I know, too, how their mothers weep and how their families sorrow."

1966

- April 12: B-52 bombers are used for the first time against North Vietnam. Each B-52 carries up to one hundred bombs, dropped from an altitude of about six miles. Target selections are closely supervised by the White House. There are six main target categories: power facilities, war support facilities, transportation lines, military complexes, fuel storage, and air defense installations.
- August 30: Hanoi announces China will provide economic and technical assistance.
- October 3: The Soviet Union announces it will provide military and economic assistance to North Vietnam.

1967

- August 9: The Senate Armed Services Committee begins closed-door hearings concerning the influence of civilian advisors on military planning. During the hearings, Defense Secretary McNamara testifies that the extensive and costly U.S. bombing campaign in Vietnam is failing to impact North Vietnam's war making ability in South Vietnam and that nothing short of "the virtual annihilation of North Vietnam and its people" through bombing would ever succeed.

1968

- January 23: North Korea captures the USS Pueblo (AGER-2). This is an American ELINT and SIGINT Banner-class technical research ship (Navy intelligence) which was boarded and captured by the Democratic People's Republic of Korea (DPRK) in what is known as the Pueblo Incident or alternatively as the Pueblo Crisis or the Pueblo Affair. Occurring less than a week after President Lyndon B. Johnson's State of the Union Address and only weeks before the Tet Offensive, it was a major incident in the Cold War.

- August 21: The "Prague Spring" was a period of political liberalization in Czechoslovakia during the era of its domination by the Soviet Union. It began on 5 January 1968, when reformist Slovak Alexander Dubček came to power, and continued until 21 August when the Soviet Union and members of its Warsaw Pact allies invaded the country and crushed the revolt.
- March 31: President Johnson announces he will not seek a second term.
- November 8: Richard M. Nixon defeats Hubert H. Humphrey and is elected the 37th President of the United States.

1969

- July 20: Apollo 11 astronauts Neil Armstrong and Edwin "Buzz" Aldrin become the first humans to walk on the moon.

1970

- March 5: Nuclear Nonproliferation Treaty comes into force. There are 189 signatories.

- April 30: President Nixon stuns America by announcing U.S. and South Vietnamese incursion into Cambodia "... not for the purpose of expanding the war into Cambodia but for the purpose of ending the war in Vietnam and winning the just peace we desire." The announcement generates a tidal wave of protest by politicians, the press, students, professors, clergy members, business leaders, and many average Americans against Nixon and the Vietnam War. The incursion is in response to continuing Communist gains against Lon Nol's forces and is also intended to weaken overall NVA military strength as a prelude to U.S. departure from Vietnam.

1971

- June 13: The New York Times begins publication of the "Pentagon Papers," a secret defense department archive of the paperwork involved in decisions made by previous White House administrations concerning Vietnam. Publication of the classified documents infuriates President Nixon.
- July 15: President Nixon announces he will visit Communist China in 1972, a major diplomatic breakthrough.

1972

- February 21–28: President Nixon visits China and meets with Mao Zedong and Prime Minister Zhou Enlai to forge new diplomatic relations. Nixon's visit causes great concern in Hanoi that their wartime ally China might be

inclined to agree to an unfavorable settlement of the war to improve Chinese relations with the U.S.
- May 26: SALT I, the first series of Strategic Arms Limitation Talks, extended from November 1969 to May 1972. In a summit meeting in Moscow, after two and a half years of negotiation, the first round of SALT was brought to a conclusion on May 26, 1972, when President Nixon and General Secretary Brezhnev signed the ABM Treaty and the Interim Agreement on strategic offensive arms.
- September 1: The Cold War is waged across a chess board. American Bobby Fischer defeats Russian Boris Spassky in Reykjavik, Iceland, to become world champion at an activity the Russians had traditionally dominated.

1973

- January 27: U.S. involvement in the Vietnam War ends when the United States and North Vietnam agree to a cease fire.
- September 11: U.S. supported coup overthrows Chilean government.
- October 6: Egypt and Syria attack Israel; Egypt requests Soviet aid.

1974

- August 9: President Richard Nixon resigns as President of the United States.

1975

- April 17: North Vietnam defeats South Vietnam.
- July: The Apollo–Soyuz Test Project (ASTP) (Russian: Экспериментальный полёт «Союз» — «Аполлон») (Eksperimantalniy polyot Soyuz-Apollon) flew. It was the last Apollo mission, the first joint U.S./Soviet space flight, and the last manned U.S. space mission until the first Space Shuttle flight in April 1981.

1976

- January 8: Chinese Premier Zhou Enlai dies of cancer.
- February: Soviet and Cuban forces help to install Communist government in Angola.
- March 24: Coup d'état in Argentina. A Civil war against Argentine-based guerrilla warfare starts.
- July 20: U.S. military personnel withdraw from Thailand.
- September 9: Chairman Mao Zedong dies.

1977

- January 1: Charter 77 is signed by Czechoslovakian intellectuals, including Václav Havel.
- January 20: Jimmy Carter becomes President of the United States.
- June 6: U.S. Secretary of State Cyrus Vance assures skeptics that the Carter administration will hold the Soviet Union accountable for its recent crackdowns on human rights activists.

1978

- April 27: President of Afghanistan Sardar Mohammed Daoud's government is overthrown when he is murdered in a coup led by procommunist rebels.
- December 25: A Communist regime is installed in Afghanistan.

1979

- January: Shah of Iran overthrown. Demonstrations against Mohammad Rezā Shāh Pahlavi began in January 1978. Between August and December 1978 strikes and demonstrations paralyze the country. The Shah left Iran for exile in mid-January 1979, and in the resulting power vacuum, Ayatollah Khomeini returned to Tehran to a greeting of several million Iranians. As a result, CENTO dissolves.
- January: U.S. and China establish diplomatic relations.
- June 18: Soviet General Secretary Leonid Brezhnev and President Jimmy Carter sign Salt II in Vienna.
- November 4: Islamist Iranian students take over the American embassy in support of the Iranian Revolution. The Iran hostage crisis lasts until January 20, 1981.
- December 24: Soviet forces invade Afghanistan.

1980

- July 28: In protest to the Afghan invasion, the United States boycotts the Moscow Olympic Games.

- August 31: Polish shipyard workers strike and form a Solidarity Union. Strike leader Lech Walesa is elected as the head of Solidarity. It is the start of a wave that would spread across the entire Eastern Bloc.

1981

- January 20: Ronald Reagan becomes the 40th President of the United States. Reagan is elected on a platform opposed to the concessions of détente.
- January 20: Forty minutes into the Reagan Presidency, the Iran hostage crisis ends.
- August 19: Libyan planes attack U.S. Navy jets in the Gulf of Sidra, which Libya has illegally annexed. The navy shoots down two Libyan jets.
- October 27: A Soviet submarine, the U137, runs aground near the Swedish naval base at Karlskrona.
- November 23: The U.S. Central Intelligence Agency (CIA) begins supporting anti-Sandinista Contras.
- December 13: Communist Gen. Jaruzelski institutes martial law in Poland in an attempt to crush the Solidarity Trade Union and political opposition.

1982

- February 24: President Ronald Reagan introduces the "Caribbean Basin Initiative" to prevent the communist overthrow of regional governments.
- April 2: Argentina invades the Falkland Islands, starting the Falklands War.
- May 30: Spain joins NATO.

- June 6: Israel invades Lebanon to end raids and clashes with Syrian troops based there.
- November 10: Leonid Brezhnev dies.
- November 14: Yuri Andropov becomes General Secretary of the Soviet Union.

1983

- March 23: President Reagan proposes the Strategic Defense Initiative to use ground and space-based systems to protect the United States from attack by strategic nuclear ballistic missiles. The initiative focused on strategic defense rather than the prior strategic offense doctrine of mutual assured destruction (MAD). The Strategic Defense Initiative Organization (SDIO) was set up in 1984 within the United States Department of Defense to oversee the Strategic Defense Initiative.
- September 1: A Soviet Su-15 shoots down Korean Air Lines Flight 007, with 269 passengers, including U.S. Congressman Larry McDonald.
- October 25: The United States leads an assault on Grenada with over one thousand troops. The force also consisted of three hundred additional troops from the Caribbean. President Ronald Reagan authorized the attack because of possible links to the Soviet Union and Cuba. The military forces find documents and weapons stockpiles that proved the connection.

1984

- December 16: British Prime Minister Margaret Thatcher meets Mikhail Gorbachev at Chequers. The "Iron Lady" finds he is someone with whom she can do business.

1985

- March 11: Mikhail Gorbachev becomes leader of the Soviet Union initiating a campaign of openness called "glasnost" and restructuring called "perestroika."

1986

- April 26: Chernobyl disaster. The worst civilian nuclear incident in history. It is a pivotal moment, exposing not only the secrecy of the Soviet regime, but also the extent to which its might is a charade built on a rickety infrastructure.
- Gorbachev ends economic aid to Soviet satellites.
- October 11-12: At the Reykjavík summit, Reagan and Gorbachev come close to a deal on nuclear arms control. Gorbachev is recognized in the west as the most sympathetic Soviet leader it has seen.
- November: The Iran-Contra Affair is revealed to the public.

1987

- June: Gorbachev *formally* announces the dual policies of glasnost and perestroika.
- October: Reagan and Gorbachev agree to remove all medium and short-range nuclear missiles from Europe.

1988

- May 15: The Soviet Union begins to withdraw its troops from Afghanistan.

1989

- January 20: George Herbert Walker Bush becomes the 41st President of the United States.
- January: The Soviet Union completes its withdrawal from Afghanistan.
- June3-4: Chinese troops massacre protesters throughout Beijing. Reports show that the theatre of the massacre spanned across the city and was densely concentrated on Chang'an Avenue, literally the "Forever Peace Street," or the main approach to Tiananmen gate where citizens returned to locate missing protesters driven from the square hours before. Video footage shows the military repeatedly opening fire here on unarmed citizens and medical personnel advancing toward Tiananmen Square to locate the missing and assist the wounded.
- June: Poland declares independence.
- October 18: Hungary opts for free elections. In East Germany, Erich Honecker resigns as head of the GDR.

- November 9: The Berlin Wall falls. East Germany allows unrestricted migration to West Germany.
- November 28: Czechoslovakia's "Velvet Revolution" climaxes when the communist regime announces the end of the one-party state. Vaclav Havel becomes president a month later.
- December 3: Gorbachev and Bush declare an end to the Cold War.
- December: Communist governments fall in Czechoslovakia and Bulgaria.
- December 25: Romania. After mass demonstrations, communist dictator Nicolae Ceausescu and his wife, Elena, attempt to flee the country. Both are captured. Within two hours of their capture, they are tried, convicted of treason, and executed.

1990

- January 31: McDonald's opens a restaurant in Moscow.
- March: Lithuania gains independence.
- October 3: German reunification!

1991

- February 25: Foreign and defense ministers of the countries of the Warsaw Treaty Organization meet to close down the pact.
- June 12: Boris Yeltsin elected president of the Russian Soviet Federative Socialist Republic with 57% of the vote.
- August 19: Attempted Soviet coup against Gorbachev. It fails but brings Boris Yeltsin to world prominence.

- December 25: Gorbachev resigns as President of the Soviet Union.
- December 26: The Soviet Union dissolves.

PARTY CENTRAL

As mentioned elsewhere, we occupied a seventh floor (top floor) apartment in the Düppel apartment complex located in the borough of Steglitz-Zehlendorf, the southwestern section of the city. Our place became a sort of "party central" during our first tour. Those parties were not always wild bacchanalian affairs. Oft times, they were calm even sedate celebrations. Although we held too many to count, we'll mention two of the more interesting to show yet another way the nation's best relaxed.

FRÖHLICHE WEIHNACHTEN!

Many of our soirées centered round a large, multi-course meal. One such event was a Christmas Day meal we held for nearly a dozen single members of Charlie Flight. We were enlisted people of rather meager means; consequently we couldn't afford to provide a feast along with presents under the tree for each person. Edie, my brilliant and resourceful wife, found about twenty boxes of pick-up sticks. She quickly snatched up enough for everyone who would celebrate Christmas at our home.

The meal progressed wonderfully. Edie had outdone herself and as always happened the single guys devoured every ounce of turkey, dressing, cranberry sauce, bread, gravy, pie, and ice cream, whatever wasn't nailed down. In addition, the gang consumed copious amounts of good German beer and white wine. I can remember being concerned about the rapidity with which my supply of adult beverages was being diminished. Frankly, I didn't think the party would last much past dessert. Happily, I was wrong.

After dinner, we cleaned up and had the singles open their present. What was intended as a "gag gift" purchased so that everyone would have something under the tree, became something much different. As each man opened his sticks, the sounds of delight increased. What surprised me were the friendly challenges that were issued time and again. The gauntlet having been tossed and picked up numerous times, a consensus of sorts was reached and a "sound" plan hatched. We would have a tournament. Edie came up with some delectable edible prize for the winner and runner up and a result's sheet with brackets and tournament rules. After mere minutes, tables and floors were cleared, competitors chosen and games begun. There was one problem. It seems the boys were competitive but in no state to compete effectively. Virtually all of them were suffering the effects of too much German cheer, be it wine or beer. They had over imbibed and no matter how much they concentrated, their coordination was off.

The game is for two or more players. Its object is simple enough, pick up the most sticks. To begin the game, a bundle of sticks is dropped from a few inches above a table or floor so that they end in a randomly tangled pile. The more tangled the resulting (dis)array, the more challenging the game. In some versions of the game, any isolated sticks, or sticks lying alone, are removed. The first player attempts to remove a single stick, without moving any other stick. In some versions of the game, player uses a tool to move the stick away from the pile; this "tool" is one of the sticks, held aside before the game begins. In other versions, players must pick up the sticks by hand. In either case, players must not move any other sticks while attempting to remove the chosen stick; if any other stick moves, his or her turn ends immediately. Players who successfully pick up a stick can then have another turn; the player keeps removing sticks until he or she causes a secondary stick to move. The game is over when the last stick is removed. The winner is determined by the highest amount of sticks picked up.

Obviously, the game requires rather intense concentration, a scarce commodity at this particular meal. We had to come up with a cure. Coffee! As each critical match began and progressed, the call went out from first one, then two, and finally all competitors. "We need some coffee, and we need it now! Please! Bitte!" The game had become more important than the party. The formerly rowdy, group was completely silent, lost in concentration over a blue, yellow, or red stick. Surprisingly, increasing sobriety was welcome; something highly unusual for this particular crew on holiday, especially when the wine and the beer was provided by the host. It was as difficult to grasp as the thought of a college student refusing a free meal. My former concern about the then rapidly decreasing supply of adult lubricant gave way to the same concern for the rapidly decreasing amount of coffee in our kitchen.

The scene before us was incredible. Contests were so intense that neither Edie nor I dared move across the floor. I remember being thankful that there was an extra restroom down the hall from the kitchen. We watched in awe. No one dared move suddenly. Nor did anyone dare to raise their voice. It would have been laughable had any of the combatants been less than dead serious about the game and the result. Men in our profession where chosen because of their ability to intercept and accurately analyze the communications of our communist neighbors. The job required intellect, nerve, sobriety, intuition, and maturity. In a few short hours, these intelligence experts were transported back to a simpler, less complicated time when a mere game occupied their complete attention. We've celebrated many Christmas dinners since, but I still look back on that afternoon and evening as one of the best ever.

As Edie busied herself baking "trophies" and begging neighbors for additional coffee, I was enlisted as a referee—a dangerous position with pride and prestige at stake. If you've ever actually played pick-up sticks, you know that the game takes ten to fifteen minutes max. Well, not this tournament. Competitive instincts took over and games droned on. I broke up more than one friendly altercation and was called upon to adjudicate several complaints. I remember being thankful that every judgment I levied was accepted without complaint or challenge. Eventually, a winner was declared, and to my eternal surprise, accepted. Although I have pictures of the event and remember each person who attended, I cannot for the life of me remember who won. By game's end, Edie had made enough goodies so that everyone was able to take an edible memory of the event home. Truth be known, it didn't matter. Guest after guest thanked us profusely. We were more than pleased. Even though the event lasted to midnight, Edie and I admitted that it could have gone longer. No booze—no fights—just good, clean fun.

EIN GLÜCKLICHES NEUES JAHR!

Every year as the clock nears midnight on December 31st, the eyes of America turn once more to the dazzling lights and bustling energy of Times Square, New York. Anticipation runs high reaching climax as the infamous ball begins to drop. As exciting as that overcrowded parcel of concrete and neon is, it couldn't match the drama and incongruity that accompanied New Year's Eve in West Berlin at the wall.

For our pick-up-stick Christmas, we had invited mostly single servicemen and women. On New Year's Eve, we invited our married friends. Our reasoning was simple, on Christmas you miss family, but on New Year's you want to party. I don't remember how many couples attended this particular celebration, but everyone was dressed to the hilt. In the early 70s, glitter was the height of fashion, and our guests succeeded in outdoing any fireworks show I'd ever witnessed.

I won't go into detail. Suffice to say that we outdid ourselves in the consumption of food and adult beverage. As the party progressed, Edie put out a large bowl of Screaming Yellow Zonkers. They weren't the hit we thought they would be. During the party, someone shoved a firecracker deep into the bowl, and it exploded before I could get to it. After the eruption/explosion, we had Zonkers stuck to each wall and the ceiling. Partygoers seemed to enjoy them more served in this fashion than from the bowl. For the remainder of the evening, people would retrieve the eye-level snack and casually pop it into their mouths.

The use of fireworks by one brought out the stash that couples had smuggled into the apartment. As one, we all moved to the balcony to set them off. That's when we were attacked by teenagers with bottle rockets from the playground seven floors below. Suddenly, a number of rockets appeared on the balcony. The game was on and the battle joined. We fired several salvos at them and they returned the gesture at us. The building took several hits with some enemy rockets disappearing into balconies below. One of our friends attempted to toss a large cracker when it exploded in his hand. Miraculously, he emerged unscathed. My right ear was less than a meter from the explosion, so I was effectively deaf for the remainder of the party. The shot that ended the battle occurred when a bottle rocket flashed up from the playground, flew over the balcony wall, shot through the open door, and exploded on our apartment wall. Edie and I were the only ones upset about the damage, and the party continued.

At midnight, we again moved onto the balcony to throw the last of the fireworks. As on other New Year's Eves, the border guards on the East Berlin side of the wall decided to join in the celebration. Since atheists don't recognize Christ or Christmas, this evening was their only noncommunist celebration, and celebrate they did. While we watched, they shot off some of the ordinance at their disposal. We saw several trip flares turn night sky into day. We also counted at least two rather large explosions that shook the balcony and several patrons. Some of our battle savvy veterans thought they sounded like mines. Lastly, several of our group swore they heard automatic weapons fire, a definite "no-no" for guards at the Wall. It was exciting and eerie and surreal and typical all at the same time.

We had many parties, but that Christmas and New Year's remain two of the more memorable.

NERVES OF STEEL AT THE HELM

Pan American World Airways operated mostly in the Central Air Corridor flying into Tegel as well as Tempelhof.

Soviet pilots regularly harassed allied aircraft in an attempt to force a violation of the air corridor borders or even get one of the crafts to land. Harassment began during the Berlin Airlift and never really ceased until reunification. Soviet activities in the air were sometimes augmented by East German assistance from the ground. While the Soviets were flying precariously close to allied aircraft, the East Germans would attempt to disorient allied pilots with high powered spot lights aimed at their cockpits during their final approach to Tempelhof. These attempts occurred so regularly they were often the subject of magazine and news articles. Three such reports appear below, two from the annals of *Time Magazine* and one from a declassified *CIA Intelligence Memorandum*.

1. Time Magazine 23 March 1962: "I'm flying two meters above him. Now I can see his expression, and he can see mine...I wave him down...He waved back...He did not move...Can I get permission to shoot him down?"

These were the radioed words of a Soviet fighter pilot buzzing a western transport plane in the skies near Berlin. Failing to get a reply from his Russian ground controller, the pilot did not fire. However, the message, monitored by U.S. authorities, was evidence of dangerous new tensions in Berlin's aerial war of nerves.

"On and off for several weeks, the Russians have been sending up fighters to harass western planes. Last week, the Reds announced dozens of air corridor flight plans that would put Soviet transport planes at precisely the same altitudes at precisely the same times previously allocated to western aircraft. This maneuver turned out to be sheer bluff; the Russian flights usually were canceled at the last minute, or the pilots simply chose a distant, safer course. But Moscow now tried another nuisance technique.

"Radar operators in the West Berlin air traffic control center were startled to find unusual pips showing up on their scopes. The signals were too small to be airplanes, much too concentrated to be a rainstorm. They were, in fact, reflections from great batches of aluminum chaff dumped into the sky by high-flying Soviet planes. The idea, presumably, was to test new ways of confusing the flow of western planes."

"From a technical standpoint, the radar harassment was no major threat to today's sophisticated electronic gear, which allows skilled operators to see through such outmoded forms of jamming. But the west was concerned at the continual harassment. Noticeably annoyed, President Kennedy called dropping the aluminum chaff 'a particularly dangerous kind of action.' The U.S. seemed more determined than ever to fight if the Russians nudge too hard in the corridors. U.S. jet fighters, armed with Sidewinder missiles, recently have been aloft at the western end of the Berlin air lanes, ready to reach the scene of trouble in minutes. Giant U.S. C-133 Cargomasters, capable of hauling huge trailer trucks, began practice runs up to West Berlin in case an airlift might soon be needed."

"Doubletalk: At Geneva (see above), U.S. Secretary of State Dean Rusk and British Foreign Secretary, Lord Home, made Moscow's rough stuff over Berlin Topic A in their first talks with Russia's Andrei Gromyko. As reported by the New York Herald Tribune's Marguerite Higgins, there ensued some uncommonly blunt words among the three statesmen. Andrej Gromyko, 'I know nothing of the difficulties you mention in the air corridor.' To which Dean Rusk replied, 'May I observe, Mr. Foreign Minister, that if there is a gap in your information, it could easily be rectified by one quick call to the Soviet Ministry of Defense in Moscow?' Unruffled, Gromyko, insisted, 'And may I be permitted to observe, Mr. Rusk, that it is improper for the American secretary of state to tell the Soviet foreign minister how to conduct his business?' Ever irascible, Rusk continued, 'Mr. Gromyko, I have noted of late that Mr. Khrushchev seems to be speaking with two voices. One, Mr. Khrushchev is the man of peace. The other Mr. Khrushchev is the one who makes the decisions in the air corridors. From now on, I am going to listen with two ears to establish which the real Mr. Khrushchev is.'"

2. "Time Magazine 3 July 1964: Flying some of the cold war's hottest routes, Pan American World Airways meets political turbulence as often as the natural kind. Pan Am hardly inaugurated its new thrice-weekly New York-Berlin service before Moscow thundered that the nine-hour jet flights violated four-power agreements on Berlin and warned darkly that it could not be responsible for any dire consequences. Predictably, the airline kept right on flying last week, and the Communists did nothing."

"Although the Russians have long harassed Pan Am's flights from eight West German cities through the 110-mile air corridor to Berlin, its Berlin run has become one of the most traveled, most curious, and most profitable air services in the world. Pan Am's internal German service is the biggest of three flown into Berlin by the Western allies (the West Germans are banned by the four-power treaty); British European Airways and Air France also operate into the divided city. The U.S. flag carrier gets 60% of the business, largely because it has the most flights. Currently, Pan Am has 44 round trips daily, hauls 2,000,000 passengers a year. The load factor is an airman's dream: 70%."

"Tourists & Tinsel: Business generates itself. To demonstrate West Berlin's viability, the West German government encourages festivals and scientific seminars there; and to stimulate travel, it pays the airline subsidies up to 30% on each ticket. West Berlin businessmen, doing 80% of their business outside the city, shuttle continuously by air to West Germany. For foreign tourists in Germany, the Berlin Wall has become a sightseeing must. Pan Am, flying 15 older DC-6Bs that are more economical than Air France's Caravelles or BEA's Viscounts, profits handsomely on yearly revenues of around $15 million."

"There are lumps in all that gravy. Pilots descending toward Tempelhof airfield at night have been deliberately and dangerously blinded by East German spotlights. Their navigational aids, essential in a political corridor only twenty miles wide, have been knocked out by tinsel strewn from Russian planes. Worst of all, MIG fighters have buzzed the commercial planes or escorted them wing tip to wing tip in an effort to unnerve pilots. 'Crisis,' sighs one Pan Am executive, 'is a way of life.'"

"Beards & Bans: To keep morale flying high in that way of life, Pan Am operates its 'airline within an airline' with reckoned informality and a tolerant disregard for some rules that bind most other air crews. The 166 flight crewmen, some of whom have flown the Berlin run for more than a decade, have a certain derring-do, and Pan Am even allows them to cultivate combat-veteran beards. The 109 German stewardesses are permitted to fly after they marry. Indeed, many are married to their own pilots."

Even our colleagues at the CIA saw the need to report on Soviet harassment in a January 1968, Top Secret, since declassified, memorandum. In it, the CIA reported that a British Military Transport was forced to land even though it was flying well within the Berlin corridor.

One such incident produced a hero of sorts. A Pan Am aircraft flying though the Southern Corridor from Frankfurt am Mein to Berlin suddenly picked up an unwanted escort of East German MiG-21 fighters. It seems on this occasion, the East Germans wished to force another aircraft to land as they had the British Transport. In order to insure such a resolution, the pair of fighters was more aggressive than usual. The story goes that the MiGs positioned themselves mere meters above each wingtip of the hapless Pan Am. When the Pan Am pilot seemed to pay little or no attention to the Soviets, they became indignant and motioned with their hands and by wiggling their wings that the airliner should begin a slow but deliberate descent.

That's when the actions the Pan Am pilot took became legend and part of the lore told and retold about Berlin and the Wall during the Cold War. If the tale is indeed correct, he gazed to his right and left taking note of each fighter pilot and their insistent almost frantic gestures. Unfazed, he then made a gesture of his own to each with the middle finger of first his right and then his left hand. Apparently, he was ambidextrous. If this weren't brazen enough, the captain made a great show of putting the plane on autopilot after which he pulled a newspaper out of his flight bag, propped his feet up on the console, and began to read as if he were sitting on his couch any Sunday morning. For the remainder of the flight, the pilot totally ignored the increasingly perplexed East Germans. I'm sure their conversations with ground controllers lit up the airways. To the dismay of the co-pilot, passengers, and the East German fighter pilots, the Captain ignored every attempt to regain his attention. He wasn't just ignoring the MiGs; it was as if he became so disinterested in their attempts that he seemed to forget they were there. This indifference lasted all the way to Berlin, where the pilot casually refolded his paper, yawned and stretched his arms high into the air, looked to each MiG and saluted smartly, disengaged the autopilot, and began preparations for final approach and landing.

If the pilot received any reprimand for his actions, it did not accompany the tale. What did come forward was the gratitude and admiration of the crew, passengers, and GIs such as me who have told and retold the tale for decades. It seems that everyone either knew of or had experienced Soviet or East German harassment in the past and had had more that their fill. The pilot and the tale passed into legend although its veracity cannot be determined with any accuracy.

EDIE FORGES EAST BERLIN

For the wives who could travel to East Berlin, the situation was almost absurd. Come to think of it, the Cold War rarely made sense. They lived behind the Iron Curtain in West Berlin with husbands who spied on the East, yet they were allowed to cross the border at will and shop in the "People's Paradise." Edie crossed Checkpoint Charlie into the east several times. This is her account of the first.

A shopping trip to East Berlin was not a spur-of-the-moment decision. To begin, we would apply for entry passes at Berlin Brigade, which might take two weeks to process. Also, we would have to exchange our money. The bank at Tempelhof Central Airport would exchange dollars to West German Deutsche Marks (DM). In 1971 the rate of exchange was roughly 3.68DM to each $1.00 (It would plummet to 1.70DM to $1.00 within four years). We would then go to one of several banks near Checkpoint Charlie where we would exchange our west marks for east marks (Ostmark, OM) at the rate of one west mark for four east marks. This was done "under the table," because the East Germans demanded that Americans purchase their east marks in East Berlin where the exchange rate was a paltry 1DM to 1OM. Because of that regulation, we always saved a few DM to exchange upon entry into the East. When we arrived, we would do the nominal exchange while saving the paperwork to "doctor" later with pens of various colors and intensity, which we had brought for just that purpose. All purchase receipts, which were presented to and scrutinized by the East German border guards, had to equal the amount exchanged at the hotel, with the exact OM in change remaining. I must note that west marks were printed on quality paper, and its coinage was stamped out of nickel and like metals. They felt heavy in your hand. Their counterparts in the East were printed on cheaper paper with their coinage stamped out of tin. A good breeze could, and would blow it away. Rarely were our receipts closely checked, but we always had to be prepared for an East German crack down.

My mentor in forgery was Jean. She was a veteran of many shopping forays into the East and was a pro at forging the exchange slips and purchase receipts. A native of Scotland, she was a delight. Fortunately, everything then was handwritten. There were very few machine-printed register receipts, especially in the East. Jean and I would match the color and intensity of ink, copy the handwriting, and change the amounts on the receipts to match our purchases and the amount of East money we had left. After all, exchanging our DM for OM in the West allowed us to quadruple our buying power while claiming the one to one exchange rate that was permitted. We gave thought to the consequences, which might include detention, interrogation, and a stay in an East German prison, but only when we found ourselves close to discovery.

My first time driving into East Berlin was frightening. We were so closely watched—every pass was checked and checked again—even our trunk and back seat was dismantled and searched. After that introduction to the freedoms of communism, we crossed over through Checkpoint Charlie. This was no small feat for the checkpoint was not a straight road, it was three curves (a rough S) interrupted and surrounded by barricades, towers, and heavily armed guards. The hair pin turns encountered were built to prevent a straight, high-speed dash by some would-be defector through the checkpoint. With that gauntlet behind us, we headed for Alexanderplatz and its famed hotel where we would officially exchange our marks. To my surprise, exchanging money at Hotel Alexanderhaus was as uneventful as exchanging money at Tempelhof.

After exchanging marks at the hotel and obtaining the paperwork we would later doctor, we traveled to the stores I had only heard about from seasoned shoppers. We had been cautioned by our Military Police (MP) and the East German Volks Polizei (VOPOs) not to stray from a specific area designated for American travel. To do so would result in our arrest for presumably straying into sensitive areas for the purpose of espionage. We took their warnings seriously. However, one glass store we had been encouraged to visit was in a hard-to-find section of the city outside the area we were confined to. Undaunted, we decided to try and locate it. As we ventured further and further from Alexanderplatz, our anxiety increased. After driving down numerous side streets, we found the poorly marked store, parked, and entered a small, cheerless sales room. There we found only cheap, everyday glassware. Disappointed and anxious to get back, we were about to beat a hasty retreat when the proprietor motioned for us to wait until the present clientele had left. When we were alone, we were somewhat taken back when the owner quickly locked the front door. He beckoned us to follow him behind a faded curtain and through the door it concealed. Our hearts were in our throats—my first thought was that our "money-laundering scheme" had been discovered and we would never see our families again. Worse than our impending imprisonment was the thought that our actions would cause our husbands to lose their clearances! Since our introduction to the intelligence community, it had been driven into our psyche that the loss of a security clearance would hound a person's life to the grave. That fact had been reinforced so many times that it became a vivid part of our social conscience. Throwing caution and our spouses' future to the wind, we followed.

What we discovered behind that ill-repaired door was spectacular. In that drab, windowless back room with a bare bulb suspended by a single wire from the ceiling was a sight reserved for the privileged few. We found shelf after shelf of lovely, hand cut lead crystal. Our mouths dropped open as our collective heartbeat once again approached normal for the third time this day.

We determined that we could now afford the luxury of curiosity and asked why these treasures were hidden from the masses. It was akin to being in the storage area for a museum or art gallery. He replied that the others (East German residents) could not afford such pieces, and if they were to see such quality they would realize the deprivations they lived under. In fact, the shopkeeper philosophized, they were better off not knowing that such quality even existed. I suppose that that knowledge might have made them question the utopia the government insisted they lived under. He continued by telling us that he only allowed foreigners and a privileged few communist officials into this sanctuary. We made our purchases quickly. Being in that room both excited and saddened us. I felt a sense of loss for those who would never experience what I was now enjoying.

After making our selections and having them wrapped, we attempted to pay. To our amazement, the shopkeeper asked what amount we would like him to enter on the receipt! He was "in" on the scheme. He knew the game and was willing to play—so much for the utopian socialist state where "rule of law" was the order of the day. We told him what to enter and forked over our East Marks while he dutifully wrote our receipts. We left as stealthily as we had entered. Astonished, relieved, and not just a little nervous by what had just transpired, we made our way back to Hotel Alexanderhaus. We would visit this shop many times in the future.

When we arrived, it was time for lunch, which was a treat. It was always a lengthy, leisurely affair. We ordered several courses of fine cuisine, each beautifully presented. We always accompanied our meal with fine West German white wines. The food was delicious and the service impeccable with every need anticipated by a well-trained staff. The tables were covered in starched white linens, fine china, and heavy silver. The hotel's décor enhanced rather than detracted from our experience. Simply, it was an island of color and charm in the middle of the gray, drab world outside. The restaurant was never crowded, and the majority of the diners appeared to be businessmen. We presumed not all were local. When it came to pay for the experience, we were always amazed that the equivalent of two dollars bought our food, drink, and a generous tip.

After lunch, walking around the area we were allowed to travel in was always an experience. Most East Germans we saw on the street and in the shops were neatly dressed in brown or black leather; however, it was cheap leather. To a person, they also wore a somber, almost emotionless expression on their faces. The average East German adult never smiled in our presence. The way they reacted to us was always disconcerting. Not preoccupied with shopping as we were, they seemed to be aware of where they were and, more importantly, who was around them. We were reminded that in a communist state, everyone was constantly under suspicion. As a counterpoint to their parents, children wore bright colors and seemed happy and playful. They behaved and played like children everywhere. The public restrooms were not for the weak. Reeking and filthy, it was better to wait. It always seemed peculiar to me to have restrooms that would drive you back to streets that were immaculate and litter free. Again, we were in the capitol of East Berlin, the showplace of socialism with Alexanderplatz its hub. Even the buildings, although faded, poorly constructed, and painted a concrete drab tan, were clean with sparkling windows. Merchandise in the shops appeared in neat piles and rows with nothing out of place. Some shops sported empty shelves, dusted, and ready to be filled. Conspicuous in their absence were overflowing bins of goods commonly seen in the West. No less conspicuous were the lines of people. You could tell when a shipment of a scarce or desired commodity such as well-made shoes, clothing, or household items had arrived. Knowing our abundance, I just couldn't stand in those lines, no matter what was at the other end. East Germans seemed to value rather poorly made, utilitarian kitchenware. Understandably, they also valued their cheap clothing, although the leather was tanned in formaldehyde and exuded a sweet-rancid odor when warmed.

During each trip, we couldn't shake the feeling that we were being watched. Paranoid? Maybe. I know for a fact that we were followed at least once. The secret police encouraged its citizens to watch friend and foe alike and report on their activities. On top of that, undercover police were said to be everywhere there were Americans.

At the end of our shopping day, we would park several blocks from the checkpoint to arrange our receipts, make needed changes, and double check our totals. We were also careful to repack our purchases for we never knew when we would be closely inspected. Those necessary tasks done, we would take a deep breath, don happy carefree expressions, and head for Checkpoint Charlie. There we knew we would have to fool both the East German and American border guards. We had been cautioned not to be overly talkative with the East Germans. We were also warned not to move too quickly or show any excessive emotion. After all, several cameras and weapons were focused on that short gauntlet. We would exit the car and enter the first floor of the tower seen so often in photos of the checkpoint. Inside, we would present our passes to the expressionless officer who sat behind a spartan, unadorned counter. The walls were decorated with the East German flag, a noticeably retouched picture of Eric Honnecker, and whoever happened to be premier in the Soviet Union. The officer would review our paperwork carefully, write something in a ledger—presumably our names and just how attractive we were—then he would lead us out to examine the contents of our car. This might be nothing more than a quick look at the packages in our trunk and back seat, or it could be a thorough inspection of every package and the remainder of the vehicle's contents. A recent escape through or over the wall would trigger a very vigorous inspection. This was always a sobering, somewhat frightening experience. Once the official was satisfied, a relative term, for they never really seemed satisfied, he would return our paperwork and motion us through to the west. Another guard would lift the metal, red and white pole that blocked movement forward. We would drive no more than five mph through the S-curve again ever aware of eyes watching and guns at the ready until we crossed the white line (border) in the west. On the American side, the procedure was nearly the same, but the atmosphere was so much more relaxed, more "free." We would quietly rejoice when we finally encountered the Army MPs. Yes, we scammed them the same way we had their East German counterparts, but we did so without malice, almost unintentionally. The East Germans were our enemies, and putting one over on them was desired and expected when one could. If the Americans got caught in our wake, oh well, we did what we had to. Besides, I've always believed the MPs knew exactly what we were doing. I can't prove it, but I'll always believe it.

During a couple of our trips, we were interrogated by both the East Germans and Americans about where we had been, how long it took to shop in certain stores, prices, had we seen anything unusual, had we left the approved area, had we been approached and by whom, etc. However, no one ever questioned the validity of our receipts. Shopping with an accomplished forger was the only way to go. Being questioned by the Americans never left the dry lump in my throat that always appeared when I sat in front of the East Germans. I suppose we knew that Americans operated under different rules. They actually had rules. We knew that the East Germans could do whatever they wanted. The threat of an international incident was not a deterrent in a country the United States and the other western powers never recognized diplomatically or officially. In other words, they didn't exist and could do whatever they wished.

And so it went for the majority of our second four-year tour in West Berlin. I found some great buys, but my memories are not the goods I gathered, rather they recall the many exciting experiences Jean, others, and I had.

~Edie

BERLIN, THE "ISLAND CITY"

Reunification ended an era where an indigenous people were increasingly divided by two diametrically opposed ideologies. If politics was the only thing separating them, the split might not have been quite so divisive. Add to that the resulting economic disparity and eroding freedoms in the East and you can understand why the Soviet Union through its puppet, East Germany, felt compelled to act. In 1961, the East Germans constructed a wall on the border between the Soviet and the Western Zones. The ideological barrier became one of brick, concrete, and steel.

WHY THE ISLAND CITY?

West Berlin was the generally accepted name given to the western section of Berlin, Germany between 1949 and 1990. It consisted of the American, British, and French occupation sectors established in 1945 at the end of WWII. In many ways it was integrated with, although legally not a part of, West Germany. The Soviet sector came to be known as East Berlin, which East Germany claimed as its capital; however, the Western Allies did not recognize this claim. The allies asserted that the entire city was legally under four-power occupation. The building of the Berlin Wall in 1961 sealed the border with West Berlin, which since the end of the WWII had been surrounded by communist East Berlin and East Germany roughly 110 miles from West Germany. The "Island City" was born.

Officially, West Berlin was called "Berlin (West)" by the West German government, and, for most of the period of its existence,

"Westberlin" by the East German government, which suggested that West Berlin wasn't really part of "Berlin" as a whole. It was only during the period just before reunification that the government in the East began to use "Berlin (West)." East Berlin was officially called Berlin, Hauptstadt der DDR ("Berlin, Capital of the German Democratic Republic"), or simply "Berlin," by East Germans.

The Potsdam Agreement established the legal framework for the occupation of Germany in the wake of World War II. According to the agreement, Germany would be under the sovereignty of the four major wartime allies—the United States, Great Britain, France, and the Union of Soviet Socialist Republics (Soviet Union)—until a German government acceptable to all could be reconstituted. Germany would be divided into four sectors, each administered by one of the allies. Berlin, though surrounded by the Soviet sector, would be similarly divided, with the British, French, and American districts occupying the western parts of the city. According to the agreement, the occupation of Berlin would end only as a result of a quadripartite agreement. This clause did not apply to Germany as a whole. Each of the western allies were guaranteed an air corridor to their respective sectors of Berlin, and the Soviets also informally allowed road and rail access between West Berlin and the western parts of Germany.

At first, this arrangement was officially a temporary administrative expedient, and all parties declared that Germany and Berlin would soon be reunited. However, as the relations between the western allies and the Soviet Union soured and the Cold War warmed up, the joint administration of Germany and Berlin broke down. Soon, Soviet-occupied Berlin and western-occupied Berlin had entirely separate city administrations.

In 1948, the Soviets tried to force the issue. On June 24th, the USSR blocked railroad and street access to the three western sectors of Berlin that the western powers had been controlling.

Their goal was to force the western powers to allow the Soviet controlled regions to start supplying Berlin with food and fuel, thereby giving them nominal control over the entire city. The west responded by using its guaranteed air corridors to resupply the city in what became known as the Berlin Airlift. The airlift was viewed with skepticism in both the East and the West. The logistics required to supply a population of two million had never been attempted before. In comparison, the airlift to supply the German 6th Army at Stalingrad (now Volgograd) required three hundred tons per day, which was rarely achieved. The Berlin effort would require at least five thousand tons a day. In spite of this, by the spring of 1949 the airlift was clearly succeeding, and by April airlift delivery exceeded the previous rail totals.

The Airlift's success humiliated the Soviets, who had claimed repeatedly that it would not succeed. The Soviets finally relented, lifting their blockade on May 11, 1949. The future of West Berlin as a separate jurisdiction had been ensured. One of the lasting legacies of the Airlift was the three airports in former western zones of the city, which served as primary gateways to Berlin for another fifty years. Of note, Col. Gail S. Halvorsen, the famous candy bomber of that airlift, would be my commander in the 1970s.

By the end of that year, two new states had been created out of occupied Germany—the Federal Republic of Germany in the West and the German Democratic Republic in the East—with West Berlin an island surrounded by, but not part of, the latter. According to the legal theory followed by the western allies, the occupation of most of Germany ended in 1949 with the declaration of the Federal Republic of Germany and the German Democratic Republic. However, because the occupation of Berlin could only be ended by a quadripartite agreement, Berlin remained an occupied territory under the formal sovereignty of the allies. Hence, the Grundgesetz (constitution of the Federal Republic) had no application in West Berlin. Meanwhile the

Soviets unilaterally declared the occupation of East Berlin at an end along with the rest of East Germany, but this move was not recognized by the western allies who continued to view all of Berlin as a jointly occupied territory belonging to neither of the two states. As a matter of fact, soldiers assigned to West Berlin were awarded the WWII Army of Occupation Medal until reunification in 1990. I still count this medal proudly in the collection I earned during some twenty-three years of military service.

However, in many ways, West Berlin functioned as the de facto eleventh state of West Germany, and was portrayed on maps published in the West as being a part of West Germany. Inhabitants of West Berlin were treated as citizens by West German authorities, and there was freedom of movement, to the extent allowed by geography, between West Berlin and West Germany. There were no separate immigration regulations for West Berlin and all immigration rules for West Germany were followed in West Berlin. West German entry visas issued to visitors were stamped with "valid for entry into the Federal Republic of Germany and Berlin ," authorizing entry to West Berlin as well as West Germany itself. But the western allies remained the ultimate political authorities there. West Berlin was run by an elected mayor and city government at Rathaus Schöneberg, but this government formally derived its authority from the occupying forces, not its electoral mandate. As a matter of fact, the Federal Republic of Germany provided for allied military housing and other forms of support as a yearly item in its budget.

The ambiguous legal status of West Berlin meant that West Berliners were not eligible to vote in federal elections; instead, they were indirectly represented in the Bundestag by twenty nonvoting delegates chosen by the West Berlin House of Representatives. Similarly, the West Berlin Senate sent nonvoting delegates to the Bundesrat. However, as citizens of the Federal Republic, West Berliners were able to stand for election; including Social Democrat Chancellor Willy Brandt, who was elected by means of his party's list of candidates. Also, men there were exempt from the Federal Republic's compulsory military service; this exemption made the city a popular home for West German youths, which resulted in a flourishing counterculture that became one of the defining features of the city.

Other anomalies included "provisional ID cards" without the West German coat of arms, a ban on Lufthansa and any other West German airlines' flights to the city because the air corridors between West Germany and West Berlin as agreed in the post-war era were to be used by UK, French or U.S. planes only. Even without this to consider, East Germany refused to permit use of its airspace since it too claimed the Lufthansa name. With West Berlin surrounded by East German territory on all sides, flights out of West Berlin would have been logistically impossible. West Berlin had its own postal administration, separate from West Germany's, which issued its own postage stamps until 1990.

Communist countries however did not recognize West Berlin as part of West Germany and usually portrayed it as a third German jurisdiction. The disagreement about Berlin's status was one of the most important debates of the Cold War.

While West Berlin was a formally separate jurisdiction from East Berlin after 1949, there was, for more than a decade, freedom of movement between the two, and in many ways Berlin still functioned as a single city. The U-Bahn and S-Bahn public transit networks, rebuilt after the war, spanned all occupation sectors. Many people lived in one half of the city and had family members, friends, and jobs in the other.

As the Cold War continued, many East Germans began leaving East Germany for the West. East Germany closed the borders between East and West Germany in 1952, but did not seal off West Berlin, because there was freedom of movement between West Berlin and West Germany, Easterners could use the city as a transit point to the West. It was in large part to stop this drain that the East German government built the Berlin Wall, thus physically closing off West Berlin from East Germany, on August 13, 1961. It was still possible to travel from West Berlin to West Germany by air and by specific rail and autobahn transit routes set aside for that purpose, but inhabitants of the two Berlins were now physically and legally separated from each other.

The Four Power Agreement on Berlin (September 1971) and the Transit Agreement (May 1972), helped to slightly ease the tensions over West Berlin and at a practical level made it easier, though with nightmarish restrictions, for West Berliners to travel to East Germany and simplified the bureaucracy for Germans travelling along the autobahn transit routes.

At the Brandenburg Gate in 1987, President Ronald Reagan provided a challenge to the then-Soviet premier: "General Secretary Gorbachev, if you seek peace, if you seek prosperity for the Soviet Union and Eastern Europe, if you seek liberalization, come here to this gate! Mr. Gorbachev, open this gate! Mr. Gorbachev, tear down this wall!"

On November 9, 1989, the wall was opened, and the two cities were once again physically—though still not legally—united. The so-called Two-Plus-Four Treaty, signed by the two German states and the four wartime allies, paved the way to German reunification and an end to the western occupation of West Berlin. On October 3, 1990, West Berlin and East Berlin were united as the city of Berlin, which then acceded to the Federal Republic as a state, along with the rest of East Germany. West Berlin and East Berlin thus both formally ceased to exist.

A TRIP TO THE "ZONE"

As good as life could be in West Berlin, we occasionally felt compelled to take the military train or drive through East Germany to "get off" the island. This meant travel to West Germany.

During our two tours there between 1970 and 1981, we took every opportunity to make this journey. Although, we flew into Tempelhof and Tegel on the now defunct Pan American Airlines, the two methods of travel that were the cheapest were train and automobile. Each of these methods was adventurous and sometimes exciting to the extreme. I'll describe them.

Train Schedule
20 Sep 70–22 May 71

Berlin to Frankfurt
Dm 80610
Depart Berlin: 2022

Frankfurt to Berlin
Dm 80609
Arrive Berlin: 0654

Arrive		Depart		Arrive		Depart
2050		2101	Wansee	0623		0633
2113		2132	Potsdam	0542		0610
2341		2356	Marienborn	0242		0257
0008		0023	Helmstedt	0158		0230
0049	Read	0157	Braunsweig	0122	Read	0131
0201	Down	0210	Kreiensen	0018	Up	0027
0234		0236	Goettingen	2353		2355
0325		0340	Kassel	2258		2306
0450		0455	Marburg	2151		2153
0515		0530	Giessen	2126		2133
0553		0556	Bad Neuheim	2104		2106
0601		0602	Freidberg	2056		2100

Arrive Frankfurt: 0653
Depart Frankfurt: 2036

THE INFAMOUS "DUTY TRAIN"

To transport American servicemen, their dependents, and U.S. Army civilians in and out of the Allied sectors, the U.S. Army Transportation Corps established the Berlin Duty Train in late 1945. My wife and I made the trip numerous times during our two tours. The U.S. had a total of four passenger trains that traveled through Frankfurt, Bremerhaven, and Berlin consisting of three compartmentalized sleeping cars, an escort car, and a mail and freight car. The British and French had counterparts. U.S. Army trains traveled only at night, and the trip averaged nine hours, depending on time spent to check passports and orders. Approximately 80,000 people made the trip each year.

Each train that left from Berlin's Lichtefelde West station or Frankfurt am Main was assigned a train commander, a Russian-English interpreter, two Military Policemen/Policewomen (MPs), a radio operator, and a conductor. The train commander was almost always a transportation corps lieutenant, who was responsible for the safety and security of the train during its journey. No one was permitted to get off the train at checkpoints, except for the commander, interpreter, and senior MP. Passport inspection by the Russians took about an hour and if information did not match exactly—a period, comma, or a space in the wrong place—a person could be and sometimes was rejected.

U.S. Army Transportation Corps personnel used several timetables for their military trains. The "duty trains," as the nightly U.S. Army passenger trains were called, kept to a strict timetable with frequent and lengthy stops in addition to the familiar border crossing stops at Wannsee-Potsdam and Marienborn-Helmstedt. The complexity of the schedule and frequent delays accounted for the nine hours travel to transit the 340 miles from Berlin to Frankfurt Am Main.

Maintaining the schedule was of critical interest to all concerned, both from the army standpoint and that of the operator, the Deutsche Reichsbahn. The train had to meet other trains at the right sidings, and had to maintain its position in the "parade" of overnight sleeping car trains carrying civilians. This was mostly carried out with obsolete equipment.

We always questioned the rationale for traveling at night when our British and French allies traveled during the day. The explanation I heard concerned the Army's desire to keep the trip from becoming a vacation. Military leaves or passes began at midnight. A soldier would board the train on while still officially on duty. He wouldn't begin to leave until after falling asleep. However, on the return trip, the same soldier boarded while still on leave but arrived the next morning on duty.

As stated, the British Military Train operated on a different principal. It made a day round trip from Berlin-Charlottenburg to Braunschweig and return. This led to the provision of dining car service, and offered the best sightseeing of East Germany.

The purpose of its timing, however, was to connect via Hannover with trains to Hoek van Holland, and from there, to the overnight British Rail or Netherlands Railway ferry to Harwich. The ferry was met by the express Boat Train to the Liverpool Street Station in London. This pattern was reversed in the eastbound direction.

The French Train Militaire faced yet another set of requirements. It had the most elegant schedule, but thanks to the demolition of railway lines between the French Sector of West Berlin and East Germany, their trip from and to Berlin-Tegel took hours of stop-and-go operation, following S-bahn trains in some cases. The effects of this were eased by tasty food from a bistro car, washed down with Alsatian beer.

By extending the train across the border from Kehl, in West Germany, to Strasbourg, now in France, this service offered the possibility of traveling all the way between Berlin and France without having to speak German. Due to the small size of the French garrison in Berlin, it only operated triweekly.

To give you some insight into a trip on the U.S. Army duty train, I've provided the following schedule from the early 1970s. Note the numerous stops. I'm a light sleeper, and I awoke every time the train halted and recommenced its journey. The train was wonderful, but I always arrived in Frankfurt needing a nap.

There are memories of our duty train travels that are indelibly etched in our minds. Operated by the Transportation Division of the U.S. Army Berlin, the duty train used to transport allies in and out of Berlin was in a word, magic. To be sure, any airport in the free world was abuzz with activity. But, the duty train seemed almost clandestine in its mission. We were still enamored with and very intimidated by the Iron Curtain. Any trip though this physical and mental barrier was certain to get adrenalin flowing.

Army green railway Pullmans left every evening from the Berlin-Lichterfelde West railway station (in German Bahnhof Berlin-Lichterfelde West). It also served the Berlin S-Bahn and several local bus lines. The station was built in 1872 in the style of a Tuscan villa as a train station for the elegant development of Villenkolonie Lichterfelde West, a newly created expensive residential area for wealthy Berliners. It served as the terminus of the duty train from 1946 until 1993.

I distinctly remember the little restaurant across the street, I believe it was called the Macedonia, where Edie would enjoy a Berliner Weisse mit Schuss and I would order a doppelbock before we boarded the train. As you can see by the schedule, we did not tarry. The train left precisely on schedule and made its assigned stops as written. If it did not, our antagonists and supposed allies would begin their harassment. I remember clearly that our flag orders had to be letter perfect with no strikeovers, cross outs, or smudges. If they were not perfect, we could be denied travel.

Our accommodations were not as Spartan as one might imagine. There were two beds, the one above pulled down and the one below served as a couch/seat. The linens were freshly starched. There were feather pillows and warm woolen blankets. The room was roughly five by eight and was connected to another bedroom by a fascinating lavatory. The little lavatory was mahogany from floor to ceiling with stainless steel fixtures. The stainless toilet sported a mahogany seat. Above this was a polished mahogany door atop a mahogany cabinet that when opened, revealed a pull-down stainless steel sink with a mirror above. The room itself was small with barely enough room to turn around, but it was so well appointed that it made the trip a little easier and more elegant. When both doors to the lavatory were open, we could carry on a conversation with the occupants of the other room, which we did often.

We spent many evenings on that train being lulled to sleep by the rhythmic clakity-clack of wheels on rail as we rolled through the pitch-black countryside. As the schedule depicts, stops were frequent and were announced by the screeching of brakes. Even the drowsiest passengers woke when the train came to a halt. Over the rushing air from the brakes and the shouts of conductors and engineers, one could hear the voices of MPs and Soviet guards comparing each flag order and U.S. Army Pass Folder against the manifest. It was at such a stop that Edie, created a memory the family still enjoys to this day. Propping herself up on one elbow, she pulled the shade back a few inches as she had done numerous times this trip. Not seeing the Soviets or East Germans, she scrutinized the platform and station. It was then that she observed that this must be a huge city for we'd made three stops in the same town. Curious, I asked what the name was. She replied, "Ausgang." After my laughter subsided, I told her that ausgang is German for a pedestrian exit. She had only been in Germany for two months, so the mistake was one anybody could make. However, our garage has a German ausgang sign, which I liberated from a train platform sometime later.

In the final analysis, the duty train was the great equalizer. It was unique to the time and the situation. It served liberators who found themselves besieged by a real barrier to freedom. It gave those liberators an opportunity to occasionally break free and travel to the real world. What a time! What a memory! What a concept!

The Berlin Duty Train made its last run in December 1990, and the Transportation Corps Museum at Fort Eustis, Virginia, claims they have a Berlin Duty Train car on display. Reportedly this car was renovated for such service but was never actually used on the official run. It still carries Deutche Bundepost (German Post Office) markings, not U.S. Army and the TC branch insignia.

DRIVING TO THE "ZONE"

We drove to the Western Zone of Germany or simply, the Zone, several times. Since the memory of those trips has fused into one continuous recollection, I'll combine the experiences and construct a single experience out of the many.

Border checkpoint Alpha is in Helmstedt-Marienborn. Helmstedt is a city located at the eastern edge of the German state of Lower Saxony. It is the capital of the District of Helmstedt. Helmstedt has twenty-six thousand inhabitants. In former times, the city was also called Helmstädt. It developed in the vicinity of the Benedictine St. Ludger's Abbey that was founded around AD 800 by Saint Liudger as a missionary station. Helmstedt was first mentioned in 952, it became a city in 1247. It belonged to the Abbacy of Werden until 1490, when it was bought by the Duchy of Brunswick-Luneburg. From 1576 to 1810, the University of Helmstedt was located here.

From the late 1940s to 1990, the town was the site of a major border crossing between the Federal Republic of Germany and the German Democratic Republic. The main rail and autobahn route between West Germany and Berlin, across the GDR, began at the Helmstedt-Marienborn border crossing, also known as Checkpoint Alpha. Official military traffic from NATO countries to West Germany was allowed to use only this route.

Less well known than Checkpoints Alpha and Charlie, Checkpoint Bravo was the gateway into Berlin from West Germany. The counterpoint to Checkpoint Alpha, Checkpoint Bravo was situated on the primary road link to West Germany, which consisted mainly of the A2 autobahn.

While the actual drive was only 110 or so miles, personnel driving from Berlin to the Federal Republic had to contend with traffic and unforeseen delays. The trip, including processing through four required checkpoints, took approximately three hours before we reached the West German border. The only authorized route for American privately owned vehicle (POV) travelers driving to or from the zone was the Berlin-Helmstedt Autobahn.

The U.S. Army Europe published a regulation, USAREUR 550-180, outlining suggested and mandatory actions one was to take prior to attempting the drive. We were encouraged to take tools, tire changing equipment, extra fuses, and a full tank of gas. The first required stop was the Allied Checkpoint Bravo, located approximately 2.5 miles outside of Berlin on the East German border. Several signs announced the traveler's approach and the checkpoint building itself was a well-marked, one-story structure with flags of the three Allied nations flying above it. It was hard to miss, unless weather or darkness obscured the markings. As the other checkpoints, it was manned by American, British and French Military Policemen. Checkpoint Bravo was manned by one MP in charge and a detailed MP who monitored travel from Helmstedt to Berlin and reverse.

At the checkpoint, we presented our flag orders as authorization for travel along with my military ID card and dependent passports. We also had to produce a current vehicle registration. Before we were allowed to move on to the next checkpoint, the army had to establish that the automobile was in good mechanical condition. Travelers then received a thorough briefing from U.S.

Army Military Policemen. MP instructions typically included the correct route of travel to Helmstedt and processing procedures at the Soviet checkpoints. We were then shown the map that showed the route from Berlin—south of Potsdam through Bravo on the A2 heading southwest of Brandenburg—north of Magdeburg on to Helmstedt-Marienborn. We were encouraged to ask any questions regarding our journey before leaving the checkpoint area. We were also briefed on reporting East German or Soviet troop movements we might witness during our drive. We would deliver our report at the next American checkpoint.

Before I continue, let me say a word or two about flag orders. It was an official document issued by the U.S. Army Berlin to military members and dependents who desired travel from Berlin to the zone or vice versa. If they were not perfect, the Soviets could and would create all kinds of difficulty for travelers on the road or duty train. This mainly took the form of nit picking the documents for any form of error. No errors would be allowed or the documents would be rejected and transit refused until they were corrected. If you had a moustache, it had to be on the ID card or shaved off. They could have no strikeovers, no extra spaces, no white out, etc. They were a real pain for clerk typists using 1970's issue typewriters.

Before we left Checkpoint Bravo and drove to the first of two identical Soviet Checkpoints, the MPs warned, "Your drive should take two hours. If you make it in less than two hours, you were speeding. If it takes longer than three and a half hours, you probably took a wrong turn. In that case, we'll have to send someone out after you." As an aside, I knew some soldiers and airmen who would wait in the parking lot just so they could speed down the corridor. The MP then handed us "breakdown cards" in case our car stalled or broke down. If pulled over by the East German police, we would ask to see a Soviet officer. We were never to interact with the East Germans.

The MPs also gave us flash cards written in German, Russian and English. The first one said "I wish to proceed without further delay." The second simply said, "I demand to see a Soviet officer." Having done that, you were stuck in place until one arrived.

The Soviet Checkpoints in East Germany were sterile and foreboding. After transiting a bleak, no-man's land, we would pull into the Soviet Checkpoint on the East German border near Dreilinden. The entire area was a few hundred yards long and shaped in a rectangle surrounded by a huge chain link fence. An unseen guard would electronically open the gate at the narrow edge of the rectangle. We would enter and drive slowly forward. The huge floodlit area was empty of people and vehicles—very eerie. Procedure dictated we stop in front of a solitary Soviet soldier standing near a sentry box not unlike the ones manned by palace guards at Buckingham. Upon exiting my car, I marched smartly toward the guard, whereupon we would exchange salutes. Rank was not important; the salutes were intended to be friendly gestures between Allies. It was unusual at best, because each guard was a member of the KGB, people I rarely considered allies.

The guard then walked slowly around my car, checked that the registration number, the license plate, matched the details on our Flag Orders, and then handed the papers back to me. We exchanged salutes once more when he would then indicate that I should walk over to a small hut about across the street. Not a word was spoken. There was a strict rule concerning photography. Simply, it was forbidden in any form. Violation of this or any directive carried with it penalties ranging from detainment to incarceration. Undaunted, my wife chose to violate the rule and took a picture. It shows a KGB Border Guard in a Soviet Army uniform saluting me as I approached with our Flag Orders. It seems Edie had planned the entire thing without my knowledge. She had hidden a small Kodak 110 camera in her purse in anticipation of this moment. Had she been caught, the camera would have been confiscated and everything and everyone searched. She had to be quick, because the guard would walk around the vehicle immediately after taking our documents. Fortunately for us both, she got the picture without rousing even the slightest suspicion from our inspector. If everything checked out, I was directed to the building across the driveway. I remember being thankful that the office window was blacked out.

 Inside the building, I pushed my documents through the familiar semicircular hatchway. The window above the hatch was shuttered as usual. While pushing my paperwork through, I would bend in an attempt to see the rank of the officer and staff inside. The waiting room measured some ten by fourteen feet. It was decorated with two somber pictures of Lenin and Brezhnev. A meager selection of English and Russian language magazines and newspapers lay on a cheap, well-worn table. Conscious of the CCTV camera staring down on me from the ceiling in a corner, I ignored the Russian literature and picked up an English-language magazine and sat down to wait. Normally, travel documents came back through the hatch within a couple of minutes, warm from the photocopier and authenticated with a Russian stamp. But on some occasions, the wait was interminable. One such incident caused the MPs at Helmstedt to come out looking for us. The Soviets delighted in one-upmanship. This time, they decided to sit on my Flag Orders. After thirty or so minutes, I decided to amuse myself. On the door leading into the office where my persecutors were biding their time and mine hung a sign stating "Дежурный По Комнате" or "Officer of the Day." It was fastened with four Philips-head screws. With nothing else happening, I decided to gather a souvenir of my inconvenience. Unfortunately, even though I had been rather stealthy, while removing the last screw the door flew open and a lieutenant colonel with a scowl that would curdle milk ripped the sign from my hand. I attempted to explain it was loose and I was merely trying to refasten it. I don't think he believed me, but I do believe he understood my hasty English.

When my papers were eventually thrust back through the hatch, I saw that my rescuer was none other than the Soviet army lieutenant colonel who had retrieved his sign. He surprised me with a curt, "Thank you, have a pleasant journey," in excellent English. I left without a word. The guard checked to see that the documents had been stamped with the Soviet authorization to proceed and then handed them back to me. We saluted again and I got back into my car. I made note of the time knowing I ["we" instead of I] would never arrive at Helmstedet when we were expected. The U.S. Army would be worried and no matter how greatly I broke the eighty kilometer per hour speed limit, we were destined to be late.

Those next two hours were stressful. The road was a single lane each side for most of the way and passed through several forests and sparsely populated areas. Although one of the main thoroughfares thru East Germany, the road needed serious repair. It was festooned with potholes and sported crumbled shoulders. I spent much time watching my rear view mirror as my wife cradled our map on her lap. On numerous occasions, we noted the movement of East German and more rarely Soviet convoys. Upon arrival at the Soviet checkpoint, the procedure was the same as at the Berlin end.

However, one such return stands out. After the formalities, the outside guard leaned closer and asked in somewhat curious Russian, "Имейте Вас кое-что, что Вы желаете обменяться?" or do you have anything you want to trade? Allied servicemen sometimes traded objects of interest with our communist counterparts for Soviet ephemera or uniform items that interested us. Over the course of six years, one of my friends managed to build an entire uniform. Obviously, this type of fraternization was strictly against regulations. I attempted to ignore his question, but I must not have been very convincing as the sentry pressed on. Eventually I pretended to cave and bartered a *Playboy* I had purchased for just such an occasion for a Soviet belt buckle. It so happened we were transporting friends who were visiting from the states back to catch their plane in Frankfurt. They hadn't experienced communist shenanigans before and had seen way too many James Bond flicks. John was somewhat taken back when I produced the buckle upon entering the car and instructed him to place the magazine in a plastic bag and throw it at the feet of the guard as we slowly drove off. He attempted to comply, but the Cold War and being face to face with a KGB Border Guard had softened his resolve. Instead of gently dropping the sack in place, he threw it with all his might hitting the guard squarely in the chest. The accompanying thump startled the guard and petrified my wife and friends. The exit gate at the other end of the rectangle was also operated electronically. In spite of our unintended assault, the gate began to open. It took all my composure not to floor the accelerator and made our escape. Nonetheless, the shouts of John's wife, Patty, coupled with everyone's nervous laughter resulted in a rather speedier exit than had been our entry.

Minutes later, we would enter the safety of the Allied Checkpoint at Helmstedt. There, we were to report anything unusual or any troop movements we'd observed. We always reported all troop movements and any delays or detentions. Somehow, we always managed to forget trading items with the guards, a lapse I chalk up to stress and fading memory. Besides, writing a lengthy report and answering thousands of questions would take hours of valuable break time.

Whether eventful or not, the trips were always an adventure.

ENCOUNTERS

In the course of our years in Germany, we had many memorable encounters during our travels. In the following paragraphs, I'll relate family favorites from each member. Our daughter and son enjoy telling the story of our trip to Holland and the unique way we got in and out of the country. It's with this encounter I'll begin.

EASY ENTRY, AWKWARD EXIT

We'd been close friends with a couple we had met in Syracuse at Intermediate Language School. They had two children, a boy and girl, like us, and we enjoyed similar activities and professions. For the purpose of this book, I'll call them Jim and Cathy.

We had decided to take a family trip to Amsterdam during one of our infamous breaks. Edie and I wanted to take the kids to Madurodam, the Van Gogh Museum, Rijksmuseum with its spectacular Rembrandts, Delft Factories, and the Anne Frank House.

As usual, we got duty train reservations, purchased tickets for all the connections to Amsterdam, and packed everything needed and not needed for the trip. We got the first sergeant and his family to take care of our wonderful cockapoo, PD (short for Pierre D'Artagnan), and set out on our journey.

The duty train was uneventful. The kids were so excited that sleep came later than usual, but their joy buoyed them throughout the trip. We made our connection in Frankfurt without a hitch. The kids slept as the magnificent Germany countryside passed by. Edie provided our normal travel lunch, which consisted of cheese (Swiss or Edam), apples, good German brötchen (bread), and apple juice for the kids and German white wine for the adults. It was always special, and the fact that we were once again on the road made it more so.

On the way, we had to change trains. This occurred in small town somewhere near the border with Holland. I can't remember the name of the berg, but I do remember that the town seemed to be quite a distance from the bahnhof (train station). While I was attempting to determine when our connecting train would arrive, Cathy commented that we eight were the only ones on the platform. That got the kids talking about being in the middle of nowhere and speculating on our chances of making our connection. My German is not good, but I was able to communicate with the station master (Bahnhofsvorsteher). I began to question my ability when I heard him say that we had missed our connection and there wouldn't be another train to Amsterdam until the next morning. Responding to the look of disbelief and confusion on my face, he repeated himself in his best and measured English, "Your train gone...no more today."

The news did much to dampen the mood of both families. At first, no one believed me. So, I asked the station master one last time. Somewhat exasperated, he showed me my ticket, the connection on the posted schedule, and the fact that we had missed it by nearly an hour. He was right and we were stranded. *Would we lose our reservations and deposit in Amsterdam, would we be able to find a gasthaus and restaurant in this town, and would we be able to make it back to Berlin in time for our next shift?*

It seems our train from Frankfurt had been delayed three times during the trip north. We were having such a good time, we didn't even notice. It was true. We were stranded and now had to find rooms for two families and attempt to make connections the next day. The prospect was not one we entertained with any measure of eagerness.

It was at this awkward moment that the station master approached us with a suggestion. It took quite a while and much use of our German/English dictionary, but he explained that an engine would be going to Holland in about forty-five minutes to bring some cars back. We would be able to make another train going to Amsterdam and arrive there only an hour or so after our scheduled original time.

There was one huge catch. The only train going to Holland was the engine. The eight of us would have to ride with the engineer in the engine compartment. We gathered that it would be wise to offer the engineer something for his generosity if he even agreed to take us. That meant we were in for some dickering. There was very little discussion. We agreed.

The engine showed ahead of schedule. The station master flagged the engineer down from his cab and began a lengthy and animated discussion of our situation. I have to admit that we were more than nervous in anticipation of the engineer's response. After what seemed like an hour, the station master introduced us to the engineer and explained that he would be happy to take us for $20 American and two bottles of wine. We agreed with one stipulation, we had to be able to catch the next train to Amsterdam. After more discussion, we agreed to his terms and paid our fare.

It was tight, but the eight of us complete with luggage managed to fit in the cab. The kids were fascinated with the gauges and levers and the fact that we were so "high up in the air." The engineer climbed aboard and our adventure began. It would not be a long trip, but it was worth at least twice what we paid. Our driver turned out to be an old softie. He blew the whistle on a child's command and even allowed the kids to blow it a couple of times. They were thrilled, and we all enjoyed the open-air cab. It was a beautiful afternoon and a great antidote to our problem.

As we drew near the border, the engineer became more and more serious. As we got within a kilometer of the Netherlands, he shot a glance at me and shouted, "Bitte, jeder, herunterkommen," while motioning us to the floor with his hands. His tone and glimpses out the window at the border needed no translation. He wanted us all to get down, now.

Edie understood his tone and sign language instantly. She shouted, "We're crossing the border without authorization. If anyone sees us, we could be detained and even arrested."

With that, we hit the floor and motioned the kids to be quiet. With the engineer's increased tenseness, my adrenalin began to flow. I wasn't concerned for myself, but I didn't want our kids to remember the day I got them arrested. They seemed to understand the seriousness of the situation; they were as quiet and motionless as they had ever been. You could tell by their expression and the width of their eyes that they were exited and scared at the same time. It was a long few minutes. After a safe distance, our benefactor relaxed and with a smile motioned us to get up. We were less certain than he, and it took us a bit of time to rise to full height.

The remainder of the ride was fun and the wind blowing through the open cab was refreshing. All in all, we thought it a wonderful solution to our dilemma. We arrived in time to make our train to Amsterdam. The engineer even helped us board and spoke to the conductor on our behalf so that we could use the tickets we'd purchased for the trip from Frankfurt to Amsterdam, thereby saving us money and a lengthy explanation. He was wonderful and we bid him a fond farewell. The kids even gave him a warm hug as we separated.

As promised, we arrived just an hour or so late. We walked to the pension, found our rooms, and unpacked. The pension was owned and operated by a WWII survivor. He was a quiet man but quickly told us that the steepness of the stairs to the second floor was evidence that we were actually climbing to the third. The second floor, accessed by a hidden ladder in his kitchen, was used to hide Jews during the German occupation during the war.

He and his family had saved many. Incredible! As we would find out later, the Anne Frank house had a similar hidden floor.

The next day, his hospitality still at its best, he served us an excellent continental breakfast of warm fresh rolls, rich Danish butter, aromatic cheese, salami, and jam. We washed it down with his special hot Dutch cocoa.

We saw everything we came to see. The kids loved Madurodam. Edie and Cathy bought some Delftware, which we have to this day. Jim loved the boat tour of the canals. And I loved the architecture. Of course, we all enjoyed the tour of the Amstel Brewery (taken over by Heineken International in 1968).

We were all sobered by the Anne Frank house and the sad events that occurred there only three decades earlier. We even saw the best supporting actress Oscar that Shelly Winters won for her portrayal of Mrs. Petronella Van Daan. Ms. Winters donated it to the house in perpetuity.

I was amazed at the windmills, so much larger than I had expected. We even took a tour of the "Red Light District." We were shocked at the window displays of women in various stages of undress. We joked in the beginning, but left somewhat sad.

With each day, we grew less and less concerned about our manner of entry into Holland and really relaxed.

With our trip nearing an end, we determined we would not be late for our train. We got to the station early enough to get some wonderful, smooth, Dutch chocolate for the trip. We boarded and prepared for our journey to Frankfurt. Edie broke out the cheese, bread, and apples. We capped it with fine chocolate, and sat back for a nap.

Eventually, the train conductor came by to check our tickets and stamp our passports. Jim and I traveled on military ID, but our wives and children each had to present a passport. When he asked for their passports, a shudder went through the adults. The conductor examined the passports again and again. Finally, he challenged us with, "Who checked your papers when you entered our country?" His English was good, which made it difficult to feign ignorance. I fumbled some lame answer, but he was not to be dissuaded. He looked at Edie and again asked how we entered. I took the lead and began to play dumb American. In essence, I attempted to convince the conductor that there had been some confusion on the train when we entered and we had been overlooked, that plus the fact that we weren't sure if we needed to have passports stamped in the first place since Jim and I had military IDs. His expression let us known in no uncertain terms that he was not convinced. I think we all took turns trying to keep from being asked to get off at the next stop and talk to the authorities. We did blanch when one of the kids said, "We came in on a big engine!" Fortunately, the conductor was much too occupied with what to do with us to hear the truth. Finally, thankfully, he accepted the fact that we were dumb Americans and let us continue on the train. Ironically, he didn't stamp our passports either. We have no official record we ever visited the Netherlands. Thank God we have pictures.

On the way to Frankfurt, we had a wonderful discussion about the events surrounding our entry and exit. I think our relief and excitement registered with our children. To this day, our daughter, Chantelle, and son, Darby, happily tell one and all how they "snuck" into Holland.

DANISH MINELAYER

We were members of the American Yacht Club Berlin during our second tour in the city. This facility was located on the eastern shore of the Wannsee at Am Sandwerder 17-19. I'd been on Berlin's waters before as a pirate, but this would be much different. I eventually became a licensed master sailing instructor for the Red Cross. For a couple of years I also served as vice commodore.

Our best friends and worthy competitors were the British. They were great sailors and even better hosts and guests. It was through them that I first heard of the British Kiel Yacht Club4, the offshore sailing center for the British Forces in Germany. Located on the Baltic, the club was established in 1945 to teach British servicemen the art of sailing, diving, and adventure. In the 1970s, the club opened up their courses to NATO allies in Europe. Although I was not the most experienced sailor in our club nor was I the best, I couldn't pass up the opportunity. My friend Winger and I applied to take the week-long offshore hand course. To our surprise and delight, we were accepted and our class date set. We would later find out that we were the first regular American servicemen to attend the program.

We arrived in time to check in, meet our skipper, and find our boat. We got permission to board, stashed our gear, and familiarized ourselves with the boat and area. After that, we attended our orientation. I can't remember exactly how many of us there were, but we filled the club. We were informed that we would attend a soiree that evening to greet one another and meet the club's officers. We had about an hour to eat and get ready for the event. I skipped dinner and put on a blue blazer, shirt, and tie. As it turns out, I was the only other person outside of the commodore who had bothered to put anything other than oilskins on. I stuck out like a sore thumb. To add insult to injury, Winger was dressed like the rest of the British crews. It wasn't long before the commodore approached, and engaged me in conversation at the same time ignoring the others. During our exchange, he suddenly raised his voice and said, "It is indeed a shame when a Yank teaches us how to dress in our own club. I would suggest the rest of you go back to your boats and change." He then bought me a gin and continued to ask about my life in Berlin. As the crews left muttering something about "that damn colonial," I knew it would be a very long week indeed.

It was a long week, not because of my supposed indiscretion, but because the Brits are so thorough and meticulous in their instruction. It was one of the best courses I'd ever attended. The course lasted seven days, and each of the seventeen boats was manned by two or three off-shore hands, a potential skipper, and a course instructor on a twenty-seven-foot cutlass or saber class boat. We sailed the Southern Baltic under the watchful eye of our instructor and made ports with such exotic names as Sønderborg, Faaborg, Ærøskøbing, and Nyborg.

We spent the first three days in the classroom and familiarizing ourselves with our boats on the waters of the fjord. At midnight of the fourth day, every boat set sail for Denmark. After a night at sea, we successfully negotiated the passage to Sønderborg. Waiting only long enough for the drawbridge to be raised, the fleet spent a long day tacking up the channel before heading for Faaborg. After a couple hours rest there, we set sail for Avemako. Avemako is a small island southeast of Faaborg. Its harbor is a small cove where we inflated rubber dinghies and practiced paddling against a strong head wind to shore.

From Avemako, we sailed to Ærøskøbing in thirty to thirty-five knot winds. After a short stay in port, we made our final stop at Marstal. The passage back across the Baltic to Kiel was uneventful save for one German submarine that chose to surface mere meters from our port bow near dawn. It was exciting. The program took a week, and passing it was one of my finest moments, especially for a damn colonial.

Certain opportunities presented themselves after taking the program and joining the club. I availed myself of a couple, one of which was an opportunity to crew aboard the sloop Kranich. Built in Potsdam in 1900, it belonged to Hermann Goering and was acquired after WWII. A British friend of mine who was also an instructor at the British Kiel Yacht Club asked me to join him aboard this beautiful craft for a week on the Baltic. I jumped at the chance. The crew was formed and provisions acquired. We would set sail from Kiel on May 26th, 1980. We would not return until the 31st.

Sloops and other ships constructed for life on the Baltic are narrower than those intended for ocean sailing. Being separated from the North Sea by Skagerrak and the Kattegat Sea, the Baltic doesn't produce the large waves encountered on the open ocean. Rather, the Baltic produces more choppy waves than large coamers (breakers). The Kranich was sleek and long. Made entirely of wood with teak decks, it had brass fittings and a long tiller rather than the traditional wheel. It was sloop rigged with one hundred square meters of main sail. It was a joy to sail and responded well to the slightest command.

Of note was our captain's insistence that I bring four or five bottles of Jim Beam bourbon. In 1980, I could buy a bottle for less than ten dollars in our military class VI store. I didn't question him until we actually boarded the craft and began to fill our larder. When I asked him why he insisted on Jim Beam in such quantity, his answer was intriguing. Existing maritime rules of salvage on the Baltic were a bit sketchy. If we ran aground or were damaged at sea and rendered immobile, anyone rescuing us or rendering assistance would have a claim to part or all of the ship. It was commonplace to barter something else of value for the help needed. Taxation and tariff on imported alcohol in Denmark was so restrictive that one bottle of Beam cost approximately $200 at the time. I had brought aboard nearly $1000 worth of bourbon.

I won't bore the reader with the entirety of our trip. We only made couple of ports, Kerteminde and Aarhus. As always the Danes were friendly and Denmark was beautiful. One memorable part of the trip occurred during a minor blow we experienced from Keterminde to Aarhus. The skipper, an old friend from Berlin, offered me an opportunity to ride the pulpit. I had no idea what he was talking about. He explained that I would take off my oilskins and don something I could afford to lose. I would then climb over the pulpit and face forward. The crew would then lash me secure to the railing. I would then ride the bow into and over the waves. I jumped at the chance. I knew it would be as much fun as climbing the mast when healed over and sliding down the main sail. I climbed over and was tied so securely with my arms at my sides that I couldn't budge. Off we went, quartering into the waves. Everyone was screaming, but I could barely hear them for the waves and water. It was intense. I had no sense of ship behind me! I was so focused on each wave that nothing else mattered. I don't get sea sick, so I was able to enjoy the entire ride up over, down into, and through the waves. It seemed like a moment, but after fifteen or so minutes, I felt the boat swerve into the wind and go into irons. It was then that the crew unlashed me and helped me back over the pulpit. I was exhausted. I could barely move, but I was so excited that I didn't stop talking for several minutes.

It was in Aarhus where we had a remarkable experience. After tacking down their long artificial harbor, we docked next to a Danish minelayer, the Fyen (N81). She had just returned from an interesting experience, not uncommon during the Cold War.

On 18 April 1980, the minelayer left Rønne on Bornholm Island sailing south to a location in international waters roughly fifty miles east northeast of Gdynia, Poland. She was following a large Warsaw Pact naval exercise. The Fyen had followed similar exercises in the past. This time, however, it was clear that the Warsaw Pact leadership did not care for such routine monitoring.

At 1400 hours, a Soviet MIRKA-class frigate that had long maintained a distance of a few miles from the minelayer suddenly changed course and made straight for the Fyen. With a sharp turn to port, the frigate came alongside at a distance of only ten to fifteen meters.

The Danish crew put its most experienced seamen at the controls should they have to perform a sudden maneuver. The next few minutes were tense. The frigate was obviously harassing the Fyen, but no one aboard knew what the actual goal was. In accordance to international collision regulations, the ship's captain, Commander Finn Alsing, held course and speed. For ten minutes, the ships sailed adjacent to one another at fifteen knots with the Soviet slowly closing the distance. Again, without warning the frigate veered to starboard colliding with the Fyen just aft of the port bow. Whether or not the move was intentional, the result was the same, damage to both ships. The Fyen immediately checked for casualties with none endured. The crew then determined the extent of the damage and concluded the ship was seaworthy and that the voyage could continue. In response to the collision, the Soviets immediately left the area apparently ending the exercise. The Danes recovered at the Holmen Naval Station near Copenhagen.

After we docked, a group of petty officers from the Fyen requested permission to come aboard and see the Kranich. From what I gathered, they knew its history better than we did. Although a small sloop compared to their craft, they spent a good hour inspecting and touching every inch of the ship. Near the end of their visit, I decided to make a presentation to the petty officers mess. I motioned to the chief petty officer, and when he approached I gave him three of my bottles of Jim Beam. His face was beaming with astonishment and gratitude. I had just contributed some $600 in bourbon to the men of the Fyen. The crew thanked us profusely as they disembarked.

We were pleased with the visit, but after such a long sail in somewhat difficult weather, we wanted to get the boat back in shape, take some nosh, and rest. Alas, it was not to be. We had no sooner cleaned the boat and secured all the lines, when the chief petty officer of the Fyen again requested permission to board. In very broken English, he requested the honor of our presence in the petty officers mess for dinner, drink, and to view world cup football with the members of the mess. We were blown away. We eagerly accepted. As an aside, he asked what we liked to drink. Our captain gave a one word reply, beer.

We shaved, cleaned up, and put on the best clothes we had. We secured our ship and started for the Fyen. As we were on the ladder, a Tuborg Brewery truck came alongside. A petty officer shouted something in Danish to the driver and motioned us aboard. Saluting the Danish flag and the bridge, we were taken into the mess. It wasn't plush, but it was well appointed and clean and bright. We were welcomed warmly, and they made us feel like dignitaries. While we were talking, the Tuborg truck driver started to bring in case after case of beer. The petty officer who asked our captain what he liked to drink had called the local brewery and ordered a delivery! Incredible! Needless to say, we had a wonderful time. Unfortunately, we stayed well beyond the time we wanted to. We made our way back to the Kranich with barely enough time to brew some very strong coffee, change, and set sail. We would have a very long day making our way back towards Kiel.

The hangover and subsequent rough day at sea was a small price to pay for the hospitality we experienced and friends we made that day in Aarhus.

BWPSBBBT, BOWLING FOR BUSES

Life on the line at our sites could and often slip the bonds of boredom and enter the realm of the unbearable. Such was often the case at Marienfelde, especially when working mids. Our intercept racks ran in a couple of long rows adjacent one to another with a voice controller walking the line reporting any input to our surveillance and warning center. This worked beautifully when the Eastern powers were up and flying; however, when they were sound asleep, we sat there with less than nothing to do. We would attempt to dial up an active frequency on our radio receivers, mostly to no avail. This exercise in futility was fondly labeled, spinnin' and grinnin.' To pass the time, some of our more creative minds would create diversions that didn't violate written or unwritten standards of conduct. One such creative endeavor saw its birth with our Polish linguists.

One especially bloody mid, our floor supervisor encouraged us, some would say ordered, to find something to copy. We had spun and grinned until our fingers and bodies were numb. I remember that it was still two or three hours before sunrise and nothing, not even a bird, was in the air. Suddenly, Worm and Dusty, two of our Polish linguists, began to beat out rhythm on their position table top. It caught on, and the other Polish linguist joined in. The impromptu percussion concert was only the beginning. Presently, they started to fashion instruments out of whatever materials they had within arm's reach. Worm made a drum, and Dusty made a kazoo. Being half-Polish and seated directly next to Worm, they asked me to join in, which I did with glee making a tambourine. This went on for the next two mids until we had fashioned a full line of instruments, and had enlisted yet another band member, a Morse intercept operator or "ditty bop" as they we affectionately called them.

The supervisor who had ordered us to find activity in the air that didn't exist had the last name of Wetzel. More than once, he expressed his displeasure with the band. When displeased, he had a way of punctuating his remarks with a low guttural sound that reminded us of a bee buzzing. In reaction to his fussing, we decided to up the ante and name the band. Dusty used the buzzing sound, Wetzel's name, their linguistic preference, and our creation and came up with the "Buzz Whistle Polack Stomp Blues Band." Beautiful!

When work was finished and we were sure nothing else was happening, the boys would break out their instruments and jam—with my addition and that of one of our token ditty bops, we had five permanent members.

As fortune would have it, we hit five just before our bowling league started—it wasn't a huge leap to add bowling team to the name of the band. Thus the Buzz Whistle Polack Stomp Blue's Band Bowling Team was born. I believe I was either secretary or president of the league that year, so the members of the team asked me acquire bowling shirts. Immediately, I fired off letters to every American brewery that came to mind. I may have exaggerated our plight a tad. I explained that we were poor servicemen stuck behind the Iron Curtain working under the most difficult conditions, etc. Along with my rather pathetic plea, I sent nicknames and sizes of our teammates. Predictably, I received quite a few letters sympathizing with our situation and explaining why they could not help at this time; however, they did not forget to encourage us to buy their beer. Two breweries, however, responded by sending us shirts. One was Pabst who sent nice light yellow shirts. The other was Pearl Beer who sent very expensive bright red King Louie shirts with our names over the front pockets and BWPSBBBT across the back. I guess they couldn't fit the full name of our team. I was more than surprised at the response, and all of us were thankful. What was so amazing was the fact that we couldn't even find Pearl Beer in West Berlin.

After our last swing shift, we made our way back to Tempelhof for our first league match. We bowled after the last swing shift so that we could stay up most of the night and get enough sleep just before the first mid the next evening. We sure looked good in our new King Louie's. Much to our pleasure, we were the object of well-deserved envy. Unfortunately, our bowling never brought the same reaction. The bowling lanes were constructed on the sixth floor, the top floor of the main terminal, and were located some seven plus stories above a below-ground motor pool. To get there, we either climbed six flights of stairs with our sixteen-pound balls or used the paternoster.

A paternoster or paternoster lift is a passenger elevator that consists of a chain of open compartments that move slowly in a loop up and down inside a building without stopping. Passengers can step on or off at any floor they like. They were easy use to when lucid and sober. They were less so after three games and any number of beer frames[2].

First built in 1884 by Londoner J.E. Hall as the Cyclic Elevator, the name paternoster was originally applied to the device because the elevator is in the form of a loop and is thus similar to rosary beads used as an aid in reciting prayers. Paternosters were popular throughout the first half of the twentieth century as they could carry more passengers than ordinary elevators. They were more common in continental Europe, especially in public buildings, than in the United Kingdom. They are rather slow elevators, thus improving the chance of jumping on and off successfully. Today, in many countries the construction of new paternosters is no longer allowed because of the high danger of accidents and because they are considered unsafe.

Well, our league continued without event for several months until one evening when a couple of our more notorious Charlie Flighter's got more boisterous than usual. It seems that Animal was having considerable difficulty keeping his ball from leaving split after agonizing split. Truth be known, a preponderance of beer frames may have been more the cause than lack of skill. Back then, we included enough beer frames to keep the bowlers lively and lubricated. It seems one of his opponents became more and more critical and antagonist with each miscue. That opponent was our good friend Reptile. He was not known for his reserve and restraint. Frankly, he was known for being somewhat loud and larger than life. So, his comments increased in frequency, volume, and vehemence.

Animal's anger grew in intensity with each verbal jab. Those who knew these two recognized the fact that Animal was rapidly approaching his breaking point. The inevitable finally happened, he lost his composure completely and all the while glaring and swearing at Reptile took his bowling ball to the window, a twelve-foot open transom deal, and threw it out.

As soon as the ball dropped from Animal's hands, he realized what he had done. Seconds before, he had been homicidal and far from sober. When he turned back from the window, he was sober and wide-eyed scared. The sixteen-pound missile that had not hit anything solid all evening descended at thirty two feet per second. To our collective amazement, it went through the roof and lodged in the floor of a new, blue Mercedes sixty-five passenger bus. We could hear the crash and subsequent thud far above the carnage. I don't remember what frame we were in let alone what game, but I do remember that our evening at the lanes ended rather early that evening.

The manager of the lanes had so much to do, he paid little or no attention to what was going on. He literally had no idea what had happened. So, when the inevitable investigation commenced, he could only say that a league may or may not have been there when the ball was dropped. Of course, we weren't talking. When the report was eventually filed, it stated that the incident occurred sometime after 3:00 a.m., well after our hasty departure. Since this was not the first time the flight had been in trouble, we had learned to deflect accusation and interrogation. That notwithstanding, we walked on egg shells until another incident drew the attention of the office of special investigations. Fortunately, at that time in Berlin, incidents were commonplace.

We had dodged another bullet—or would that be ball?

WHAT TYPE OF ICE CREAM DO YOU LIKE WITH YOUR HIJACKING?

What follows is pieced together from reports official and otherwise concerning the hijacking of a TU 134 from Gda sk, Poland to Tempelhof Central Airport, West Berlin on August 30, 1978. The details are, to the best of my knowledge, accurate.

We had just returned to Berlin after a four-year hiatus at Fort George G. Meade, Maryland, where I had worked as an instructor at the National Cryptologic School.

On that beautiful August morning, Edie and I had decided to take the children to Tempelhof for some ice cream. The ice cream parlor was a makeshift affair with windows that overlooked the loading/unloading point for aircraft arriving and departing Tempelhof. We all enjoyed the hustle and bustle of air travel. The history of this airport made the view all the more exciting.

We boarded a U.S. Army Mercedes shuttle bus at Berlin Brigade bound for Tempelhof. We never tired of looking at West Berlin in all its history and bustle and glory. We arrived at Tempelhof around 9:30 a.m. and made our way to the parlor. We intended to make a day of it after some ice cream. We would then check mail before traveling to the Post Exchange back at Berlin Brigade.

We walked through one of the many arches that housed offices above and climbed the stone stairs to the ice cream shop. Our kids always enjoyed sitting by the windows with their generous sills. Eventually, they would hop up on the sill and watch as plane after plane disgorged its contents only to allow dozens more to climb ramps to take their place. The enormous overhang prevented any glare that might be present from hampering their unobstructed view of the action mere meters from the window.

We entered just before 10:00 a.m. and ordered our cones. As always, the kids were excited to order whatever flavor and size they wanted. We moved to the window to enjoy our bounty and the view. We looked forward to a few minutes of quiet while we enjoyed our ice cream.

Suddenly, the flight line, taxi way, and entire airport erupted in activity. Alarms sounded while USAF Air Policemen and West Berlin Police began running with guns drawn to and fro in the general direction of the ice cream shop and taxiway. We had no earthly idea what was happening, but I'd been through enough alerts that I was able to differentiate this as real almost instantly. My desire was to get my family out of harm's way, but being adjacent to the main entry/exit to the runway; we were in place for the duration. There was no other entry or exit. So, I ordered more ice cream and we craned to see what we could. The kids thought this was the greatest day in the world. And, for some it was.

Eventually, we saw the cause of the commotion. A Polish LOT, LO 165, scheduled to travel from Gdansk, Poland to East Berlin's Schönefeld Airport had been hijacked and landed at Tempelhof instead. Unwittingly, we had become witnesses to history. Although attempted hijackings were plentiful during the Cold War, this would be the second to last to land at the fabled airport.

As we watched in amazement, we had no idea what had happened. As a matter of fact, we would not find out until almost a decade later what had transpired an hour or so before we saw the TU-134 taxi under the overhang before us.

It seems that a group of East Germans had been thrust into an international situation when the plane they were on was diverted. They were given a choice that they'd only dreamed of, should they defect or should they remain aboard and return to their communist regime.

U.S. Air Force Security Police first greeted then arrested the East German hijacker on arrival. At that time, he was expected to be sentenced and tried by a U.S. military court. Following the hijacker's arrest, the air force returned the aircraft, its crew and those passengers who wished to resume their journey to East Berlin.

The hijacker was Hans Detlef Tiede. When he was escorted off, nine other East Germans defected with him including his accomplice Ingride Ruske and her young daughter.

If Tiede and Ruske thought they would walk away from the plane as free citizens of West Berlin, they suffered a rude awakening. The act of hijacking a civilian airliner violated international conventions long negotiated between NATO and the Warsaw Pact. For the first and only time, a U.S. court of justice was convened in Berlin to prosecute the case. Herbert J. Stern was the American judge who tried the case in a makeshift courthouse in the departure lounge of Tempelhof airport.

As he explained, "All the countries involved—the U.S., Poland, West Germany, and East Germany were signatories to an international convention on air piracy." This meant that whoever diverted a plane had to be either prosecuted at the hijacked destination or sent back to be prosecuted.

The West German conundrum cenetered on the fact that they regarded all Germans as citizens of the Federal Republic. Therefore, no one had ever been prosecuted for escaping East Germany since the wall went up in 1961, even if they had roughed up or shot a guard. For that matter, no one had ever been sent back across the border. To prosecute a case against its own citizens would constitute political suicide.

West Berlin was considered sovereign. It had a city government, parliament, judges, elected mayor, etc., but it was still an occupied territory. Post WWII allied occupation did not officially end until unification. Truth be known, the Federal Republic of (West) Germany (Bundesrepublik Deutschland) didn't want it to end. They well knew that if the Allies left, two million West Berliners would immediately become citizens of the East.

Because of the accord, the West Germans were obliged to prosecute the case, but they couldn't prosecute fellow Germans from the East. The solution was to let the Americans take over. In fact, the solution was so desirable that they insisted the U.S. handle the prosecution. There was one small glitch, there were no U.S. Courts in Berlin. The West Germans begged the U.S. to convene a tribunal for the first time even agreeing to pay all courtroom expenses to include the prosecutors, defense attorneys, and the judge.

At the time, our department of state was concerned about the safety of civil aviation and the increase in air piracy. So, while it was possible to have sympathy for the defendants, the West considered the integrity of air travel and air safety paramount. Interestingly, East Germany would only be concerned with punishing Tiede and Ruske. State appointed Stern the U.S. Judge for Berlin in anticipation of a conviction that the U.S., West Germans, and even Poles wanted.

According to Stern, the state department determined that they had the authority to define what rights the defendants had, because Tiede and Ruske were neither U.S. citizens nor on U.S. territory, but stood before an occupational court. Further, they treated Stern as an employee rather than an independent judge. Simply, they expected Stern to follow instructions. The U.S. prosecutors, taking the lead from state, didn't want to grant the East German defendants the constitutional right to a jury trial. They reasoned that a jury comprised of West Berliners would naturally acquit, making a sham of the proceedings thereby upsetting sensitive relations with the Poles, Soviets, and East Germans.

What they hadn't counted on was Stern himself. Rather than accepting State's belief that the defendants had only those rights it was willing to give them, Stern declared if a jury trial were not held he would throw the case out and turn Tiede and Ruske free. The result was a jury trial in the U.S. Sector.

After a vain attempt by prosecutors to force the defendants to plead guilty, the case against Ruske was dismissed for lack of evidence. The jury found the hijacker, Tiede, innocent on all counts except one—guilty of taking a hostage. Stern sentenced him to nine months, which was time he had already served in detention.

The hijacking and Stern's courtroom caught the eye of Hollywood. They made a movie called Judgment at Berlin with none other than Martin Sheen playing Stern.

The trial was more interesting than the hijacking itself. In 1978, no one could foresee the eventual fall of the Berlin Wall. Nor could the various communists regimes envision the possibility of their government being brought down with it. They may have dreamed of a time when travel would be unrestricted and informants were not part of the social landscape, but they dared not voice those dreams. For many, their only hope was to escape the socialist paradise. Some spent months, even years planning their escape from East Germany. No one ever dreamed of being deposited in the West through a combination of coincidence, fate, and luck, the way fifty passengers aboard LO 165 were that August afternoon. By sheer coincidence, these citizens of the German Democratic Republic were sitting in the same aircraft, which was supposed to land at East Berlin's Schönefeld Airport.

One such person was Ingrid Ruske. Working as a waitress, she was known to be a confident woman with short, blonde curls. His reason for wanting to escape was love. She longed to be with him in West Berlin. In addition to their love, he had a good income, a West German passport, and an apartment big enough for two people and Ruske's miniature poodle. When her petition to leave the country was denied, she and her lover began planning her secret disappearance. Another man, Tiede, with whom she had had an affair, was enlisted to help her. Tiede wanted to escape because he had fallen in love and had a son with the object of his affection.

They had rehearsed the plan many times. Tiede was to travel to Gdansk by train, and Ruske and her daughter would follow by air. Ruske's lover would acquire forged passports in the West and meet them at the train station in Gdansk, where they would all take the ferry to the Baltic Sea resort town of Travemünde in West Germany. The plan was simple and sound. There was only one problem, Ruske's lover and the passports never arrived in Gdansk.

It seems a friend had betrayed Ruske and informed the East German secret police, the Stasi, of the plan. They in turn launched Operation "Ferry" to prevent the group from leaving the republic illegally. Her lover took a train to Gdansk to meet Ruske. When it crossed the border with Poland, Customs Officers searched him and his baggage. Naturally, they found the forged documents. He had hidden fake Polish customs stamps in the heels of his shoes.

Ruske became nervous when her lover failed to appear and didn't answer the phone in his Berlin apartment. Had their plan been uncovered? What did the Stasi know? She and Tiede knew that they couldn't board the ferry to Travemünde without the forged passports, and they couldn't return to East Berlin, where the Stasi was presumably waiting for them. Where else could they go? They needed an alternative plan, a way to escape to the West.

Ruske already had a return ticket to East Berlin for Aug. 30, and Tiede managed to get a seat on the same flight. He bought a Mondial starter pistol at a flea market. It was about eighty years old, and it made a loud noise when caps were fired. On the evening before the flight, Ruske knelt down in a pew in a church in Gdansk and prayed to God for support.

The second plan was as simple as the first, but it was much more dangerous. Tiede would hijack the airliner to Tempelhof. Ruske would carry the relic pistol. Ruske reached the airport just in time, traveling with her daughter and a friend from East

Berlin. At the security checkpoint, a customs official found a pistol in the young daughter's coat, but she assumed it was a toy and returned it to the girl. It was impossible for Ruske to conceal her nervousness. She would sit in row six.

It took roughly seventy-five minutes for the TU-134 to travel the 393 kilometers distance from Gdansk to Berlin-Schönefeld. The plane transited the Oder River, entering East German air space. It was beginning to descend when a man in row six, Detlef Tiede, stood up and walked to the front.

The Tupolev TU-134 has room for seventy-two passengers. Its two Soloviev engines create such a din, that passengers can barely hear announcements let alone one another. The flight was not completely sold out. There were fifty East German citizens on board, ten Poles, a man from Munich and a woman from West Berlin. The crew consisted of the captain, the copilot, an engineer, a female flight attendant, two male flight attendants and a navigator who sat in the glass nose at the front of the aircraft. Even though the world was justifiably cautious of hijackers, Palestinian terrorists had hijacked a Lufthansa flight, the Landshut, eleven months earlier, the cockpit door was open. LOT, the flag carrier of Poland, apparently trusted its passengers.

Tiede walked down the center aisle. When he passed Barbara Galonska in row two, she saw that he was pressing his hands against his stomach, which led her to believe that he wasn't feeling well and was headed for the restroom. It was about 9:30 a.m. Suddenly, Tiede grabbed the female flight attendant by the hair and pressed the barrel of the pistol against her head. Shouting loudly, and speaking in German, Polish and English, he ordered the pilot to land the plane at Tempelhof. Through the open cockpit door, the captain saw what was happening. He screamed into his radio that a terrorist had hijacked his plane and in order not to jeopardize the life of the attendant and passengers he would land at Tempelhof. No one noticed that the gun Tiede was waving around was practically harmless.

The Tupolev landed at Tempelhof at 10:04 a.m. Tiede, Ruske and her daughter had reached their intended destination. Unintentionally, they had brought forty-seven other East German citizens with them who would now have to make a decision about where they would spend their future. They had landed on West German soil.

The incident was a source of great embarrassment for the Stasi, which spent the next few hours asking how on earth someone who was being so closely watched could hijack an aircraft. Where were the people from Polish intelligence? Couldn't the crew have overpowered the hijacker? It wasn't until days later that the Ministry for State Security, as the Stasi was officially known, discovered that the Poles had terminated their observation as soon as Ruske and Tiede were on the plane. The last thing they expected—a hijacking.

After the plane landed, Tiede tossed the pistol out of the aircraft door. American soldiers greeted him with the words: "Welcome to free West Berlin." To the Americans, he was a hero. He shouted into the cabin that anyone who wanted to get off could leave. Then he left the plane, together with Ruske and her daughter. An East German woman sitting in row fifteen, a radiology assistant from Erfurt, quickly made up her mind and went after them.

Some forty-six East German citizens stayed behind. In row twelve, Constanze Schröder's husband whispered that they should get off the plane. All they had to do was walk through a door.

Schröder, a pediatric nurse in Dresden, was a mother to their two children. She could hardly find a quiet moment for herself, and she was constantly on the move. At age sixteen, Communist officials accused her of being insufficiently loyal and forced her to leave high school. Her father was a pastor, which made her life very difficult. Even with all this, she had no interest in leaving. Her husband, on the other hand, was eager to get out of East

Germany, claiming that he would even swim across the Danube River to escape. They had been married for three years, but there was little left to hold it together. They had gone on this trip only because her husband wanted to show their son and daughter to friends in Gdansk. They had driven there in their Trabant, the ubiquitous, underpowered, poorly insulated East German rattletrap. Shortly before reaching their destination, the car went off the road, turned over and crashed. It was totaled. They decided to fly back to Berlin.

She hesitated. She thought, "If I get off now, I'll never see my parents again." Once in the West, would she have the courage to divorce her husband? She knew no one in West Berlin. What would she do there? But, then again, this was the opportunity of a lifetime? She reflected for a few minutes. Should they abandon everything they held dear for this chance at freedom? As suddenly as the hijacking, she jumped up and rushed to the exit with her husband and the children.

American soldiers took the rest to a waiting hall. Any who wished to stay in the West could. West German police officers and diplomats repeated the offer. They reasoned that the hijacking was proof that no one actually wanted to live in the East. Besides, it was the perfect opportunity to provoke their eastern enemy. In 1978, Americans were convinced that anyone given a choice between freedom and captivity wouldn't spend much time thinking about it.

A U.S. officer announced that those who wanted to return home would be taken to East Berlin by bus. In less than a couple of hours, they were being asked to leave everything behind—parents, grandparents, siblings, and friends.

Galonska went to the ladies' room with her nine-year-old son, Sasha. She placed him on the toilet seat and kneeled in front of him. He liked airplanes, and he very much liked traveling with his mother, but he also liked their apartment in Berlin's Prenzlauer Berg neighborhood. He wanted to go home, to his room, his books, his toys and his grandparents. He missed his friends. Sasha said he wanted to go home.

She didn't need to ask a nine-year-old boy what he wanted to do, and she certainly didn't need to do what he demanded. However, six days after the hijacking, Galonska was still a citizen of East Germany and still longing to leave the country. She was interrogated by the investigation division at the Ministry for State Security. What happened while the aircraft was at Tempelhof Airport? What happened during her stay in West Berlin? She answered their questions for six hours and fifteen minutes, and told them about the hijacker, the family that got off and didn't come back, and how they were questioned by western officials inside the airport. She said nothing about her longing and her doubts. After reunification, Galonska was allowed to see her own Stasi file, which the secret police had opened because of her contacts to artists. The file ended on Aug. 30, 1978, the day of the hijacking. The state no longer felt that it was necessary to observe her.

Of all the East German citizens on board that Tupolev, nine remained in the West: Ingrid Ruske, her daughter and Detlef Tiede; Constanze Schröder, her husband and their two children; and a couple from Leipzig. A radiology assistant from Erfurt was standing in front of East German border guards at the Berlin-Friedrichstrasse border crossing the next day, waiting to cross back to the east.

PIRATE INVASION

Charlie Flight had been ordered to stay in West Berlin during our four-day break. A rather raucous bachelor party at a notorious local bar had resulted in a rash of OSI (Office of Special Investigations) interrogations and two congressional investigations. Decorum prevents me from retelling the lurid details of the bash. Suffice to say, a number of comrades and I were in hot water up to our vaunted clearances. After a series of interrogations, our commander had been advised to keep us within arm's reach for the next few months. In other words, don't leave town.

Ever compliant, we decided not to skip town and put our commander in further jeopardy. Instead, we planned an air clearing party at home. After much debate, we reached a consensus and decided to lease a boat and sail the peaceful waters of West Berlin. So we began to plan our next adventure. The flight unanimously agreed that I would be in charge of the festivities, always a wise move on their part. After all, I had planned the party that resulted in us being confined to town in the first place. Being "in charge" meant I would have to secure a suitable craft for a party of about thirty, plan activities, impress a crew, and plan and secure suitable nosh (foodstuffs) and libation. It was a daunting task; as ever, I was up to the challenge.

I chose my closest companion on flight, Reptile, as captain. He, in turn, chose Animal as his first mate and me as a second first mate. Even though Reptile knew little about nautical protocol, Animal and I were fine with the arrangement. So a crew was formed and duties assigned.

Since Animal spoke better German than Reptile or I, he negotiated for and secured suitable grub and grog, which consisted of a case or two of potato chips and about twenty cases of courage— Berlin's finest Shultheiss and Becks Bier. Ever the pragmatist, he also secured a few bottles of schnapps and rum just in case we ran out of beer. Reptile and I found a boat and attempted to rent the scow. I had yet to become an accomplished sailor and vice commodore of the local American Yacht Club, so the owner insisted on piloting the craft himself. Besides, he reasoned, we would be plying waters that contained the East-West German Border, and he didn't want to lose his boat. His concern turned out to be prophetic and justified.

Captain and crew busied themselves planning activities and plotting a course. We would sail from the Berlin American Yacht Club, the owner insisting we not set foot in his club or approach his slip. Our route called for us to travel northeast from the Wansee into the Havel past the British Yacht Club and up to the dam and lock. Then we would travel southwest past the entrance to the Wansee down as far as the Gleinicke Brukë. If able, we would repeat the route as often as it took to consume everything we would bring aboard. Leftovers were not an option.

Like good swabs, we completed our assigned tasks with time to spare. We even managed to get the blessing of our unit commander, telling him we were going to take a boat trip to learn more about the various sectors that made up the city of Berlin; after this trip, he would never again endorse one of our schemes. In fact, we had so much time left before we set sail that I decided to establish a theme for the trip. It didn't take long to settle on piracy. After conferring with Captain Reptile and First Mate Animal, the piracy theme was deemed sound and worth pursuing. I stole freely from our slush fund—monies left over from various pools such as our annual Ghoul Pool—and set out to purchase accoutrement suitable for a crew of pirates. I was able to find several plastic flintlock pistol kits, rubber sabers, simulated leather scabbards, eye patches, sashes, and one special parrot that my faithful wife sewed to my bloused pirate shirt over the left shoulder. It had to be the left shoulder, since I would carry my trusty cutlass in my right hand.

As expected, the majority of our flight wanted to enlist in our ersatz navy. After consulting the boat owner, we settled on twenty-five pirates. The "lubbers" who weren't selected would later be very glad they had missed our maiden and final voyage.

As the launch date neared, banners and flags were made, a walking plank fabricated, epaulets secured for the captain and first mate, special guests invited, including the base chaplain, and the weather checked and rechecked. Our last few day watches were full of anticipation and much scuttlebutt about what would transpire on the high seas.

As the day of our cruise dawned, the captain and crew found themselves on the banks of the Wansee eager to try out their sea legs and cast off. Upon arrival at the club, our ship was waiting. She was a mere thirty-five feet in length, which presented our first problem. The owner was concerned not only about the number of pirates that arrived, but also by the amount of provisions we carried aboard. To make matters worse, our pirate garb gave him cause for pause. Attempting to ease his nerves, I spoke with him at length assuring him that we would neither swamp nor jeopardize his pride and joy. My consummate negotiation skills sealed the deal. In no time we prepared to cast off. Much to my dismay to mention nothing of that of the owner, First Mate Animal smashed a bottle of cheap champagne across the bow and unfurled two banners that he nailed over the ship's name, christening our sloop the HMS Sodomy. The first mate was rarely subtle, but this was a bit over the top even for him. However, the ship's company was too busy opening Schultheiss and Beck's bottles to care. So, we were named and set sail we did. I remember being pleased that our first mate hadn't had access to a cannon.

As we made our way down the Wansee toward the Havel, our base chaplain and three gamers went below deck to play some pinochle. They would stay there until our trip was cut short by the authorities some five hours later. After the cruise, the chaplain never spoke to us again.

The early hours passed quietly. The crew seemed content to merely imbibe while enjoying the remarkable shoreline of the Havel. But, as had been proved time and again, Charlie Flight did not embrace mere contentment for long. They petitioned me, the admiral, to think up some activity suitable to our present occupation, namely that of pirates on the high seas. After some thought, I remembered my good friends at the British Yacht Club not more than a league away. I quickly hatched a plan to moor at the end of their long dock and disembark, screaming and waving swords as we charged toward their clubhouse. It seemed like a wonderful idea at the time—at least our crew thought so. After all, pillaging was something we had never attempted. A couple of hundred Marks later, the owner of the craft agreed to the plan also.

The Brits were and are incredible sports. As we raced down their dock with pistols and cutlasses punctuating the air, they poured out of their clubhouse to repel boarders. After a mock battle and some hearty laughter, we invaded the club and, more importantly, its bar and made off with some fine bitters and ale. As we swaggered back to the ship, we also appropriated some lawn furniture to place on the poop deck for our comfort. We cast off and were well away when we noticed a launch screaming out of the British Yacht Club bay. Apparently, they hadn't approved of our pillaging their club. Our overloaded craft was no match for the launch, and she and her crew of three foolhardy tars were alongside our starboard side in minutes. Once there, they didn't quite know what to do. After a long moment, the foolhardy blokes attempted to board. At the captain's command to, "Repel boarders!" We gleefully chucked them into the Havel, placed a case of Becks along with their furniture in the launch, and cast it adrift. Wet and weary, the Brits safely climbed back into their launch and limped back to their club.

Flushed with our first and last success, and too much bier, we became a bit more daring. First Mate Animal thought it would be expedient and just plain fun to also attack the Wassershutzpolizei station, not far from where we had originally entered the Havel from the Wansee. Again, we screwed up our courage, gave a glass of German schnapps and two hundred more Marks to our owner and in no time we were screaming down the dock of the West German Border Police Station. In an act reminiscent of the Brits, the couple on duty poured out of the building; however, their demeanor was decidedly less jovial. To our surprise, they seemed to take particular offense at our invasion. As they appeared more able to repel boarders than we were to invade, we merely stole some more chairs and made a hasty retreat. Again, we cheerfully cast off while dividing our booty. Again, as if on cue, a launch flew out of the harbor of our recently invaded foe. This time, however, our pursuers were armed to the teeth and announced their intent with a blaring siren and a flashing red light. Being ever quick on the uptake, I predicted that they had every intention of ending our cruise. At that very moment, Captain Reptile and First Mate Animal, eyes wide as saucers, and somewhat more stable than they had been mere minutes before, shouted incoherently at me all the while pointing at the fast-approaching launch. After a quick discussion, we made a fateful decision. We would attempt to evade our pursuers.

The three of us desperately looked around for a safe harbor. Alas, none was found, but what we did find gave us an idea. As we passed to the North of Peacock Island, we noticed that we were a mere fifty to seventy-five yards from the international border (grenze) that separated West Berlin from the East. As we neared the border, we scanned the horizon for towers. The ever-present tower with East German sharpshooters seemed to be strangely, but thankfully absent. Desperately, we begged the owner to slip over the Grenze so that we might shake our persistent and closing pursuers. Horrified at the thought of entering the dreaded and deadly East, the owner stiffly refused. As panic set in, we offered all of our remaining Marks—to no avail. With few options remaining, we decided to gag and truss up our now screaming owner. With him and his incessant yelling out of the way, Captain Reptile took the helm and immediately tacked for East Berlin. The Wasserschutzpolizei fast on our stern abruptly veered away, momentarily setting us free.

It amazes me how rapidly one is overtaken with sobriety when faced with imminent death. We were no more than fifty yards into East Berlin when an East German gunboat careened from a cove near the Sacrower See (lake) at the southwest end of the Havel. I remember thinking that there was no need for a guard tower if they had a weapon like this. To our shock, a faithful crewman was attempting to clear his weapon as he bounced and rocketed toward us. As I contemplated unconditional surrender, I heard the calm and commanding voice of BT, another brilliant but disturbed flight member, bellow from the bow, "Ready, aim..." Prior to giving the command to fire, a half dozen inebriated American crewman rose above the gunnels and aimed glistening plastic flintlock pistols at the approaching craft. Instantly and instinctively, and to our collective glee, the gunboat captain turned hard to starboard tossing up an impressive rooster tail. The hard about caused the gunboat to slow, momentarily disorienting our armed assailant. Sensing that our next action would determine our collective future for the next two or three decades, Captain Reptile deftly spun the wheel to port and sped back across the border as quickly as the old tub could get us there.

As we crossed back into the West, I couldn't help but notice that our friendly West Germans had taken the opportunity to call the army military police while we were engaging our Cold War foe on the high seas. We had repelled the commie menace, but would not receive accolades for our deed. Rather, the entire crew was arrested and the three ringleaders manacled. Once our boat owner was untied and his gag removed, he implicated us even further. I was to find out later that day that my fun was just beginning.

I'll not bore the reader with details of the resulting investigation. Suffice to say, the charge that most surprised my wife was that of piracy. Due to the considerable efforts of officers and senior NCO's in my command and the several additional congressional investigations that ensued, I did not serve the twenty-five years in Mannheim Stockade recommended by the United States Forces in Europe (USEUR) Commander. I was, however, the only crewman to suffer ignominy for our actions that day. A few months later, when I returned to the states for yet another school, I was informed that my stay in the lower forty-eight would be indefinite. Our government, specifically the Department of State, thought it best to declare me "persona non grata" in Europe. They were somewhat upset that the incident resulted in some sticky negotiations and embarrassing accusations.

It seems that international incidents such as ours required diplomatic negotiations between the Soviets and the offending party, in our case, the United States. Well, the Soviets declined. It seems they wanted the U.S. to "eat a little crow" and work directly with the East Germans. The problem stems from the fact that we never officially recognized East Germany as an independent nation state. So, when the U.S. was forced to negotiate with them over our little foray into the annals of buccaneer lore, the East Germans brought the case, and others, before the security council of the United Nations as proof that they should be recognized as an independent nation.

After a few years in the land of the big BX (militarese for the United States), we returned to our beloved Berlin. I was once again in Uncle Sam's good graces. I even joined and became vice commodore of the American Yacht Club, Berlin, leisurely sailing the waters I once terrorized.

RUNAWAY TANK

Living and working in isolation, even in a beautiful and vibrant city like West Berlin, took its toll on both nerves and psyche. Those who might be emotionally predisposed to "go over the wall" occasionally did just that. The runaway in this chapter happened. It's a matter of history. However, memory fails to recall exact details as they are blurred by time and age. I apologize if I've mischaracterized the events of the day. They are herein chronicled as I remember them.

The U.S. Army, Berlin Brigade occupied several sites in West Berlin. In addition to Brigade Headquarters and the Teufelsberg listening site, four major Kasernes or barracks housed brigade personnel.

They were:

1. Named for Brigadier General Theodore Roosevelt, Jr., who received the Medal of Honor posthumously in September 1944, Roosevelt Barracks was located at Gardeschuetzenweg / Tietzenweg / Moltkestrasse in Berlin's Steglitz district. This was the same district that housed the Army Duty Train (RTO) located some four hundred yards away, following Gardeschuetzenweg to Drakestrasse, with its railway tracks stretching to West-Germany. The U.S. Army section of the huge Roosevelt Barracks was neighbored by one of the city police department's "Abschnitt45" (various German police units). They later occupied some of the historical buildings next to Augusta Platz.

Built in 1884, the barracks housed a Royal Prussian Guards Regiment who resided there until the end of World War I, when Berlin Police units took up residence. Later it was occupied by the German Army Ordinance School. The school remained until the end of World War II when American battle units entered Berlin on July 3, 1945 and confiscated the compound.

The U.S. Army 3rd and 16th Infantry Regiments occupied it from 1945 to 1950. From 1950 until 1991, it was home of the 6941st Guard Battalion—a predominantly German unit assigned the mission of providing security to U.S. installations—and other miscellaneous units, including the aforementioned German police, who occupied roughly one half of the installation. In early 1991, the Guard Battalion moved to Andrews Barracks to make room for the Headquarters of the Bundeswehr Regional Defense Command in Berlin.

Now the "Bundesnachrichtendienst" (BND) has taken over that legendary military compound. Many of its secret missions had their beginning and ending behind the old red bricks. The whole compound is video controlled as countless cameras provide security.

2. Named for Lieutenant General Leslie J. McNair, who was killed while observing front line operations in France in July 1944, McNair Barracks was located in Lichterfelde, in the Zehlendorf district between Goerzallee, "Platz des 4. July" and Osteweg. U.S. Troops first occupied the compound in 1948 after being housed in apartment buildings that hadn't been destroyed during allied bombing. Formerly, it was a huge Nazi-Army compound and once was occupied by the German "12th Anti-Aircraft Regiment."

McNair Barracks once occupied the site of the former AEG Telefunken electronics factory, a Nazi-era complex. During the WWII, research took place on several of the miracle weapons that Adolf Hitler hoped would turn the tide of the war. One of the most important products to be developed and produced in the factory was a radar-guided flak control system which could ascertain range and select individual targets.

For many years, McNair Barracks was home to several combat battalions of Berlin Brigade. Among these was the 2nd, 3rd and 4th Battalion of the 6th Infantry Regiment, 4th Battalion 18th Infantry, later renamed in the 4th, 5th and 6th Battalions of the 502nd Infantry. After the U.S Army left, the Berlin Police took over the barracks.

Sadly, at this writing, the compound is in serious disrepair and the entire rear gate area is gone. New apartments and streets crisscross the former motor pool and stockade. The main gate is also gone with new shops located where gate guards once stood. Large markets have replaced the huge motor pools. What was once the center of the post will now house a German school.

The aforementioned "4 Ring," was constructed in 1939 by Albert Speer between the McNair and a German cemetery (Parkfriedhof Lichterfelde), it was four hundred meters long and seventy meters wide. Speer wanted to construct four "ring streets" (Autobahns) in Berlin. During American occupation, this expanse saw numerous parades and ceremonies. Now, motorcycle schools negotiate obstacles where troops once marched proudly. Every Sunday, a flea market brings temporary life back to the ring.

3. Frank Maxwell Andrews played a major role in building the small U.S. Army Air Corps of the 1930s into the powerful U.S. Army Air Forces of World War II. Furthermore, he had become one of the key military commanders in the United States' armed forces. In February 1943, Andrews became the commander of all United States forces in the European Theater of Operations. In his memoirs,

Gen Henry H. "Hap" Arnold, commander of the Army Air Forces in WWII, expressed the belief that Andrews would have been given the command of the Allied invasion of Europe—the position that eventually went to Gen. Dwight D. Eisenhower. Unfortunately, on May 3, 1943, the B-24 carrying Andrews on an inspection tour crashed while attempting to land at the Royal Air Force Base at Kaldadarnes, Iceland. Andrews and thirteen others died in the crash, and only the tail gunner survived. Andrews Air Force Base, Maryland, is named in honor of Lt. Gen. Frank M. Andrews. His name also graced the 19th Century Berlin facility, Andrews Barracks. It was conceived as the Preussische Hauptkadettenanstalt, a sort of "Central European West Point." Today, the old Kaserne is used by the German Federal Government to collect and store archives. The compound's history began in 1872:

a. Prussian Cadet Academy, 1872–1920: Between 1872 and 1878, the German government constructed the Preussische Hauptkadettenanstalt. The 109 acre site, located in Groß-Lichterfelde, had not yet been annexed by the city of Berlin. Eighteen buildings, included four big Kaserne blocks, a church and the HQ building surrounded three large yards, an exercise field, and the parade ground. The huge "Idsted (Flensburg) Lion" statue overlooked the playground. Other buildings, like the economy house were located near the rear entrance on Finckensteinallee. The mess hall sat one thousand cadets. Legend holds that every German Kaiser attended this academy. A complete roster of cadets would read like a "who's who" of pre-World War II Germany, including President Paul von Hindenburg, Chancellor Franz von Papen, Reichsmarshal Hermann Goering, and Parachute General Kurt Student, among other notables. The academy was closed as a result of the Versailles Treaty in 1920.

b. Leibstandarte Adolf Hitler, 1920–1945: Between 1920 and 1933, the buildings were home to "Stabila," an official government public boy's school. It also served as a breeding ground for right-wing political activities.

From fall 1933 to spring 1934, the former PCA quartered the SA (Storm Trooper)-Stabswache "Hermann Goering", later known as SA-Feldjaeger Corps from which many were recruited into the new paratrooper units.

On December 4, 1934, Hitler's bodyguard regiment, the "Leibstandarte" took over the entire compound. It was commanded by Joseph "Sepp" Dietrich. He was one of Nazi Germany's most decorated soldiers and commanded formations up to army level during World War II. Prior to 1929, he was Adolf Hitler's chauffeur and bodyguard, but received rapid promotion after his participation in the murder of Hitler's political opponents during the "Night of the Long Knives." Dietrich was an avid hunter and race car driver; he became one of the Third Reich's more colorful personalities. After the war, he was imprisoned by the United States for war crimes and later by Germany for murder. The Leibstandarte developed into the 1st SS Panzer Division which maintained a depot at the old academy throughout World War II. Otto Skorzeny, known as "Hitler's Commando," and by Americans as "the most dangerous man in Europe," served there briefly during this period.

To meet Waffen SS standards, between 1934 and 1938 all buildings were modernized and the area of the Kaserne was enlarged to the south. It was during this renovation that two original Kaserne block buildings were demolished and replaced with more modern barracks. Bigger guardhouses were built at the new main entrance located on Finckensteinallee. Large statues were erected to flank the gate. These two, in soldiers slang, "the eternal PFCs," (Die ewigen Rottenfuehrer) are still there, covered over and filled up, to become concrete pillars. One of the gyms was modified into an Olympic size swimming pool, with a fifty meter track and a ten meter jump tower. The newly expanded southern part of the compound included a rifle range and numerous garages. Following the Battle of Berlin In May 1945, Soviet troops occupied the facility.

c. U.S. Army, 1945–1994: On July 4, 1945 American troops assembled in the parade ground of the former "Hauptkadettenanstalt," the main military academy of the German Empire, thereby assuming formal control of the American Sector. Charred letters reading, "Leibstandarte Adolf Hitler" remained above the parade ground. Military representatives of the four conquering powers attended these ceremonies. None other than General Omar Bradley represented the U.S.

Renamed Andrews Barracks, it became the home to special troops and other support elements of the U.S. Berlin Command. The 7800th Infantry Platoon, perhaps the last racially segregated unit in the U.S. Army, occupied Andrews Barracks for a time. They were a crack drill team made up entirely of black soldiers.

Between 1961 and 1966 Andrews Barracks temporarily quartered, "rotation forces" which augmented Berlin Brigade after erection of the Berlin Wall. The 8th, 24th, 4th, and 1st Infantry Divisions deployed reinforced Infantry Battle Groups & Battalions to help protect the divided city.

Of all units stationed at Andrews Barracks for more than forty years, the two especially remembered by older Berliners are the 298th Army Band and the 20th Engineer Company. The Band performed at countless public events and ceremonies while the engineers helped build playgrounds throughout the American sector. Andrews Barracks also housed Berlin Command's and later Berlin Brigade's Headquarters and Headquarters Company. Their men and women worked at the Clay HQ compound.

U.S. Forces entered Berlin as conquerors, remained in Berlin as protectors, and left Berlin as friends.

4. Completed in September 1951, Turner Barracks housed the U.S. Army's armored troops in Berlin. It received its name in February 1952 honoring SFC Charles Turner who received the Medal of Honor posthumously during the Korean conflict.

The 6th Infantry's Heavy Tank Company was the first unit to reside in Turner Barracks. Its mission was direct support of the 6th Infantry Regiment which had been activated in 1950 to occupy the U.S. Sector of West Berlin. In May 1958, Company F (Patton), 40th Armor was activated and assigned to U.S. Berlin Command, assuming the armor role. The 40th Armor troops served until 1994 with the distinction of being the only U.S. armor unit east of the Elbe River behind the Iron Curtain.

Turner Barracks was the smallest U.S. Kaserne in Berlin. The compound was square shaped, about 150 x 150 yards and was located on Huettenweg in Berlin-Zehlendorf (subdistrict Dahlem). A huge U.S. Army ammunition dump occupied the compound's rear at the edge of the Grunewald.

The barracks housed thirty or so tanks during its existence. Through the fence Berliners could watch the daily routine of heavy tanks and their crews. Until 1952, the M-26 and M-46 were visible. After that (1952-57) the M-47 was the workhorse of the 40th. In May 1958, Turner saw the first M-48. That behemoth operated until August of 1963 when the famous M-48 battle tank took over. They were eventually replaced by then state-of-the-art M60A1/A3 tanks and two M88 tank recovery vehicles.

Occasionally, tank crews test fired their .30 caliber machine guns, using blank ammunition, on the lawn in front of the arms room adjacent to the fence. That and the noisy tank engines were not viewed as a nuisance by West Berliners, rather they were considered "the sound of freedom."

In November 1989, F Company, 40th Armor expanded and reorganized. The change brought the M-1A1 "Abrams" Main Battle Tank (MBTs) Turner. The 6th Battalion, 40th Armor was activated in Berlin in October 1990. The 40th Armor symbolized America's resolve to keep West Berlin free.

Reunification signaled a death knell for the barracks. It was soon dismantled and replaced with a housing area surrounded by a small fence. A supermarket replaced AAFES Garage that stood next to the barracks.

Early Saturday, March 2, 1974, soldiers at Turner Barracks were startled into consciousness by a claxon alerting the base to an emergency situation. After bursting from the dorms in various stages of dress, they had formed up on the company lawn at the rear of the barracks. It was then that the commander informed the brigade that one of their own had possibly launched an international incident. It seems a Specialist 5th Class William A. Thompson Jr. had stolen a 50-ton M-60-A1 tank from the motor park and was currently tearing up the streets of West Berlin as he sped toward Checkpoint Charlie.

The German Labor Service guard attempted to stop the tank as it drove over the main gate on its way into the city, but being armed only with a baton and .45 pistol, he was unable to do anything but watch. Armed with a 105 mm cannon and .50 and

7.62 caliber machine guns, all three tanks were loaded with 63 main gun rounds and ample machine gun ammunition. They represented a very real threat to the residents of the city. That, of course, was serious enough, but the greater fear was that the rogue tank would attempt to enter East Berlin. Relationships with the East Germans and Russians were always tenuous; this would not improve them and might initiate heightened tension between Eastern and Western powers. During the briefing, the commander stated that two other tanks had been dispatched with orders to stop and, if necessary, terminate the renegade if necessary.

Frantic German Police and American MPs tried to warn bewildered and terrified citizens as everyone attempted to figure out where the SP 5 was going. While they were deliberating the driver's next move, he entered the Checkpoint Charlie plaza where he drove right through the pole barriers. He positioned the tank next to a guard tower and attempted to bring it down with several attempts at neutral steering, or turning the tank at a rate exactly proportional to the rate at which the steering wheel is turned.

After inflicting considerable damage to the checkpoint, the tank reentered West Berlin proper and sped in the direction of Checkpoint Bravo. It must be noted that tank tracks literally tear up and redeposit cobblestones in its wake. These cobblestones are hammered into place by hand one at a time. At this juncture, the driver "buttoned up" the tank, closing and locking all hatches. This forced him to drive by looking through the three vision blocks that were positioned around the driver's hatch. Driving at speed with only slits as a windshield is hazardous in the extreme for a rational driver let alone one who is disturbed or demented. This fact alone no doubt caused SP5 to hit and demolish several guard rails on the autobahn. Rather than risking further destruction the guards at Checkpoint Bravo, who had heard what happened at Checkpoint Charlie, threw open the pole barrier and allowed the tank to pass through. After entering the no-man's land between West and East, SP5 Thompson drove erratically putting the tank through insane maneuvers that resulted in the tank throwing one of its tracks. With the track gone, the tank came to an abrupt halt. He surrendered to his commanding officer on East German soil.

The U.S. Army recovered the tank by hastily reinstalling the track using what the tankers called the "Fort Knox rope trick." Apparently, this method allows tracks to be replaced without breaking or disassembling the track. The tank was driven under its own power back to Turner barracks with the thick pole barrier from Checkpoint Charlie impaled by the forward tow hook. It was so firmly attached that it had to be cut off with a torch. The tank was eventually repaired and returned to service. I heard an estimate of damages that exceeded $11,000.

Those of us who knew just how sensitive this situation could have been were amazed and puzzled by the lack of action or retaliation by the Soviet. As the story goes, the soldiers who retrieved the tank and the driver had a brief discussion with the Soviet officer in charge of the checkpoint. The officer understood that one rogue shouldn't cause an international incident. After all, the Russians also had a "nut" or two in their ranks. The Soviet officer said that they would be satisfied if the U.S. made good for the damages to both checkpoints.

GRUPPENREISEN

During our two tours, we enjoyed many memorable trips. From Garmish to Amsterdam to the Baltic, we enjoyed traveling through Germany and Europe. Our trips were usually family affairs with little or no drama to speak of. I remember taking Edie and the kids to Bremen on the British Duty Train for the sole purpose of having lunch at the new McDonalds. Each trip was special; however, some were more memorable than others. Here are but two.

WE NEARLY GET THE CID ARRESTED IN ZURICH

Charlie Flight was ready to embark on another exciting and educational trip. This time twenty plus had signed up to go to Zurich, Switzerland. Once again, I was tasked with making reservations for all. The task included ensuring that our Flag Orders were perfect. If there was a discrepancy, the East German Military had no reservations about stopping and detaining an entire train for a simple misspelling.

After the last day watch, we all trooped to the Military Train Station that was adjacent to the West German station at Berlin Lichterfelde West. As usual, we awaited departure at the Macedonia restaurant where we would sample local brew.

At the appointed time, we boarded the train and found our berths. I've described the train in another chapter, so I'll concentrate on the trip. On this occasion, we had several families with children; therefore, the usual frivolities were abandoned. Rather, several gathered outside of our room to share a schnapps, or other libation and generally unwind from our long shift. A close friend who now resides in the Hawaiian Islands, whom I will call Audie, was one who stayed close to our cabin. At the time, he was single and had a large crush on my wife. We got along well, and the crush was more innocent than disturbing. He was the first to notice something unusual. We would not be able to confirm his suspicions until later in the trip. An hour or so down the tracks, Audie commented that two single men appeared to be unusually interested in our movements and conversation. I chalked it up to the beauty of the wives, mine included, who graced our group. He simply stated that their interest seemed to me more focused on some of the guys than our beautiful gals. I would have blown it off as nothing out of the ordinary and chalked it up to our ingrained wariness had I not begun to notice their clandestine tendencies. They would watch, almost study, us for a time, then they would lean toward one another and discuss—what? I didn't know. The late hour, the schnapps, the good company, and the anticipation of visiting Switzerland overcame any concern I had, and I ignored them until well after we had boarded our train for Zurich at Frankfurt Hauptbahnhof.

We arrived in Frankfurt somewhat the worse for wear after thirteen or so stops in the East. After an hour or so wait, the entourage boarded our Zurich bound train. Since we were tired and the children needed rest, the first couple of hours were dedicated to getting much needed rest. As we passed through the gorgeous scenery of Southern Germany, we once again began to gather to discuss our itinerary. Since this was everyone's first trip to Switzerland, the level of excitement increased as the kilometers ticked by. Again, it was Audie who proved to be more alert than I, and for no apparent reason feigning a British accent, leaned toward me and whispered, "Say, mate. Have you noticed the two blokes at the north end of the carriage trying not to look suspicious?" I resisted the urge to glance immediately to my left (north); rather, I moved toward one of the group whose back faced the "blokes." Engaging my target in conversation, I looked over his shoulder only to find our two friends from the duty train. These two were classic. They sported closely cropped hair, sunglasses, and black windbreakers. They were clean shaven, overly casual, and quietly observant. As before, they were three compartments away from our last couple.

Smiling, I turned to Audie and replied, "Right you were, governor. Right you were." I concluded my conversation with the diversion and motioned to Audie to follow me to the other end of the car. "Do you think they're tailing us?" he asked while nodding in their general direction. Audie also loved melodramatic dialogue. "Yes, Audie, that seems abundantly evident," I replied.

"Should we do anything about it?" He asked. My simple reply was, "If we noticed them without trying, just think what the rest of crew will see as the trip progresses? Let's confront the pair, find out who they are, and settle this." Audie agreed. So, as calmly as we could we made our way past the gathering group toward our "friends" at the other end of the car.

"Greetings, gents," I said in my nicest voice. "Pleasant day, isn't it?" "Sure is," replied the older of the two. "Where you headed?" "Garmisch Partenkirchen," I lied. Their surprised look tipped them off. They knew where we were going and were taken back by my answer. "Where are you off to?" "What a coincidence, we're off to Garmisch also to do some skiing," they offered. Audie jumped in, "Ed, are you daft, Garmisch was our last trip. We're on our way to Zurich. You need to get more sleep, dude." "Stupid me! Thanks, Audie." I answered. "Sorry guys, I guess we won't see you after this."

They genuinely looked perplexed and flustered. They had no idea what to say. What was certain was the fact that they would be shadowing us for our entire trip. I decided to end the mental "tete a tete." "Okay, guys. We know you're following us. We have two questions, who are you and why are you on this train?" I won't bore you with the conversation that followed. The gist of it was that they would deny following us, we would accuse. They hedged, we pressed. So it went, thrust and parry. After fifteen minutes that seemed more like two hours, they finally admitted they were CID and were following us because we (Charlie Flight) had "done some notorious things in the past."

I admit that I was taken somewhat back by the admission. Even though our suspicions were confirmed, I hadn't prepared myself to face the fact that I was actually being followed by federal agents. It took a minute, but Audie and I finally sobered enough to acknowledge the admission. That's when I hit upon an idea; we should invite them to tag along with the crowd. It seemed the only reasonable solution. Otherwise, we would spend the next few days craning our necks and watching over our shoulders.

"Since you intend to be our shadow for the entire trip, why don't you join us?" I offered. "After all, your vaunted cover is blown, so you might as well save both of us some grief and join the party." They whispered to each other for quite a while and finally came to a conclusion. "We seem to have no choice," the tall one said. "We can't go back and you already know who we are. So, I guess we'll join you."

It was set then. We took the two agents to meet the group. Although the meetings brought about quite a range of responses from that of shock and dismay to giggles and side long glances, our personal "agents" were accepted by one and all. A member of the group offered them a couple of beers, and they became part of the gang.

The trip went very well. Zurich, Lucerne, Mt Rigi, and the whole of the country were simply spectacular. Of note is the fact that we walked across the famed Chapel Bridge (Kapellbrücke) in Lucerne, Switzerland before it was destroyed by fire in 1993. The bridge is 204 meters long and crosses the Reuss River. It was the oldest wooden covered bridge in Europe, and one of Switzerland's main tourist attractions. The covered bridge, constructed in 1333, was designed to help protect the city of Lucerne from attacks.

Inside the bridge are a series of paintings from the 17th century, depicting events from Luzerne's history. Adjoining the bridge is the 140 feet tall Wasserturm (Water Tower), an octagonal tower made from brick, which has served as a prison, torture chamber, watchtower and treasury. Today, the tower, which is part of the city wall, is used as the guild hall of the artillery association. The tower and the bridge are Lucerne's trademark, and form the most photographed monument in the country.

As was common with Charlie Flight even when accompanied by Investigative Agents, our trip was not without incident. The guys decided to have a small party in the room of one of our single men. We purchased ample supplies of Riesling X Sylvaner, a common white wine produced in German-speaking parts of the country, beer, and "Kirschwasser" which we discovered while consuming Emmentaler cheese fondue at one of the many fondue cellars in the city.

The party commenced when everyone returned from dinner at about 2030 hours. The guys hadn't really let loose in a while, so as the store of adult beverage diminished, the noise level and moxy of the gang increased commensurately. As if on cue, at the stroke of midnight the proprietor pounded on the door demanding entry. He dressed us down for about five minutes, and demanded we disperse and call it a night. Feigning ignorance of the language or the reason for his tirade, we dismissed him and continued the party. It couldn't have been more than fifteen minutes later when the pounding returned. Instead of the proprietor, two of Zurich's finest law enforcement officers entered the room. It was then that our CID boys went pale. If I hadn't been aware of their legendary toughness, I would have sworn they were about to lose dinner. Many of us had been threatened with arrest and confinement in other countries before, so this latest faux pas didn't scare us, but it did lessen the effect of the booze. We listened to our visitors and acknowledged the fact that we would spend the evening in jail if we ignored the proprietor's directives. At their demand, we then gave them our names and contact information. It was at this juncture that our investigators attempted to negotiate a treaty of sorts. Unfortunately, the constables were having nothing of it. After the CID gave the required information they made a hasty departure. I can but imagine the content and impact of the report they filed that evening. I remember feeling guilty for having included them in the trip.

As usual, we avoided arrest and permanent damage to our future. The trip ended well and we made it back to Berlin without further incident. If the Swiss police reported us to the military, we never knew it. We don't know what happened to our CID friends. I never saw them again after they left the hotel room in Zurich. I pray they kept their situation. Although, if they did, I suspect they ended up behind a desk and left field work for good.

UP THE RHEIN AND BACK AGAIN

Thirty or so of our flight decided to go on a Rhein River boat trip. It would be our first excursion up the Rhein River for Edie and me, and we were more than excited. I was chosen to lead the group, which means I was stuck with making all the arrangements, reservations, checking Flag Orders, etc. We had an uneventful overnight train trip and successfully boarded our ship in Frankfurt.

Our ship was one of the day cruisers that travel between Frankfurt and Köln (Cologne). Edie remembers that even though the boat was a "transport" and not a luxurious cruiser, the dining room boasted the very best silverware and deluxe hotel china. We enjoyed a delicious lunch of crusty bread, hearty cheeses, and fruit, all served on a beautifully laid table. Our good friend and fellow passenger, Carman, dined with us. She admired the silverware, daring Edie to join her in stealing a piece. Having had a glass of wine and feeling a bit feisty, she agreed, and slid a spoon into her purse while Carmen swept an entire place setting into hers. Months later, Edie learned the hard way that Carmen had missed getting a spoon. After a party at our apartment that Carmen attended, Edie's spoon turned up missing. Having felt bad about taking it in the first place, Edie never asked Carmen about the item, but we've always wondered if she now has a complete setting.

It was a hop-on, hop-off vessel. A traveler could purchase a German Rail Pass that allowed passage on certain ship lines. Today, a rail pass holder is entitled to travel on boats of the KD Köln-Düsseldorfer Rhein Line on both the Rhein and Moselle rivers. They are also entitled to discounted fares on the Europabus line "Romantic Road," discounted fares on the Bayerische Zugspitzbahn rack railway, and travel to Salzburg (Austria) and Basel (Switzerland).

For well over two thousand years, the Upper Middle Rhine Valley saw the transport of goods and ideas. The result is a cultural landscape unique in Europe. The Middle Rhein Valley stretches for 65 km between Koblenz and Mainz, in central Germany. As we would soon discover, the area is festooned with medieval castles, historic towns, and countless vineyards. The rocky Rhine Valley was already a major traffic route in Roman times. The twenty-five plus castles and fortresses on its banks were constructed during the middle ages. Its owners levied tolls on the roads and the river, in return for protection against robbers. The number of these tolling stations exploded during the 13th Century when there was no Holy Roman Emperor to regulate the robber barons who ran them. In addition, these barons began robbing ships of their cargoes, stealing entire ships and even kidnapping.

To combat this military threat, various nobility, knights, and Church leadership formed the Rhine League (Rheinischer Bund). It was they who held large stake in the restoration of law and order to the Rhein. Formed in 1254, the League barely let the ink dry on the founding document before they began destroying robber baron castles effectively putting them out of business. Several of the ruins we photographed were destroyed during this action.

The practice of siege, capture, and destruction of robber baron castles survived the league itself. Political strife and intrigue over the election of a new emperor and military setbacks brought the league to its own destruction. Emperor Rudolf of Habsburg used league techniques in the destruction of highway robbers. He reduced their castles to rubble and hung the highwaymen. The robber baron was never completely eradicated and even saw a revival of sorts during the Hundred Years' War; however, they never regained the power they once had.

We sailed past some beautiful scenery all the while taking roll after roll of pictures. I must have two hundred of castles alone. They were so prolific and beautiful sitting high above the river amidst endless hectares of grapes. As a matter of fact, we all wearied of photographing castles. The riverboat stopped to take on and drop off passengers several times. Our first stop was Rüdesheim am Rhein. It lies at the foot of the Niederwald on the Rhine's right (east) bank on the southern approach to the Lorelei.

First settled by the Celts before Christ, in the first century the Romans pushed into the area. Across the river in Bingen they built a castrum, a military defensive position. The Alamanni followed and then the Franks. Glass discovered in archeological digs suggests that winegrowing was an industry even then. The town's origin as a Frankish Haufendorf (roughly a "clump village") can still be seen on today's town maps. The moment Edie and I saw the town; we were taken by its beauty.

After Rüdesheim, we went a very short way down river to Bingen. Originally named Bingium, a Celtic word that may have meant "hole in the rock," it was the starting point for the Via Ausonia, a Roman military road that linked the town with Trier. In the middle of the river near Bingen is the Mouse Tower (Mäuseturm). Originally constructed by the Romans, Hatto II, the Archbishop of Mainz, restored the tower in 968.

A legendary folktale describes Hatto as a cruel ruler who oppressed and exploited the peasantry. He used the tower as a platform for crossbowmen and demanded tribute from passing ships, shooting their crews if they did not comply. During a famine in 974, Hatto horded all the grain and sold it at such a high price that few could afford it. When the peasants threatened to rebel against him, Hatto promised to feed them all. They assembled in an empty barn waiting for Hatto to bring food. When he arrived, he ordered his servants to lock the doors and set fire to the structure. As the story goes, he attributed their death cries to mice squeaking.

Of course, when Hatto retired to his castle, he was instantly besieged by an army of mice. Sure that the mice couldn't swim, he took a boat to the tower. Alas, they followed him by diving into the river by the thousands. Although many drowned, the majority achieved the island. There, they ate through the tower's doors and crawled up to the top floor, where they found Hatto and ate him alive. Quaint!

After Bingen, we traveled several kilometers down river to Bacharach. The original name Baccaracus harkens to its Celtic beginnings. With similar beginnings as the other towns down river, we'll pick up Bacharach's history in the 14th century. It became the most preeminent transfer point for the wine trade. The small ships that could navigate the Binger Loch (a quartzite reef upstream near Bingen) would transfer their barrels to larger ones at Bacharach. From then on, the wine bore the designation Bacharacher. It was granted town rights in 1356.

Heading ever north, we left Bacharach and glimpsed for the first time the fabled Lorelei Rock. On the eastern bank of the Rhine near St. Goarshausen, it rises some 120 meters above the waterline. It marks the narrowest and deepest part of the river between Switzerland and the North Sea. A very strong current and rocks below the waterline have caused numerous accidents. Apparently, the name Lorelei derives from old German words "lureln" (Rhein dialect for "murmuring") and the Celtic term "ley" (rock). Therefore, the name Lorelei translates to "murmur(ing) rock." Powerful currents and a now invisible small waterfall in the area created a murmuring sound. This, combined with the special echo the rock produces, amplifies sound giving the rock its name and the legends and tales it inspired. One such legend has dwarves living in caves in the rock. The most famous tale has a siren sitting on the cliff above the Rhine combing her golden hair. Distracted shipmen are taken by her beauty and sultry song. As they move closer, they meet their doom on the rocks. In 1837, Heinrich Heine's poem, Die Lorelei, was set to music by Friedrich Silcher. The song is well known in German-speaking lands. The celebrated Franz Liszt wrote a version of his own. When we neared the rock, we were treated to the song by thirty or so members of the Ohio State University Choir that was on tour in Europe. Their rendition was incredible and made more so by the setting.

After a couple of other stops, we docked in Koblenz. I'd gotten everyone safely on the duty train, busses, and boat. Now I had to make sure of hotel reservations, and the next day's travel. It took quite a bit of time getting everyone into their room. To my surprise, Lowell had been consuming rum all day. As two of his friends carried Lowell by the registration desk, I tossed a room key on his near lifeless chest. He would later be required to attend AA by the air force.

With everyone safely in their rooms, Edie and I decided to explore the city. We picked up a couple of friends from flight, Danny and Annette. We decided to explore Fortress Ehrenbreitstein across the river. It was built as the backbone of the regional fortification system, Festung Koblenz, by Prussia between 1817 and 1832 to guard the middle Rhine region, an area that had been invaded by French troops repeatedly before. The fortress was never attacked. The place was enormous and could be defended by up to 1200 soldiers. We took a ski lift type of chair both up and back down from the mountain. Edie is afraid of heights, so she was a real trooper to go with us. Defensive structures on this location date back to 1000 AD. The best thing about the fortress was the view offered of Deutsches Eck.

Deutsches Eck (German Corner) is the name given to a point of land at the confluence of the Mosel and Rhein rivers. A giant equestrian statue was placed there in 1897 to honor German Emperor William I. It was to symbolize German unity. The inscription quoted from a German poem read, "Nimmer wird das Reich zerstöret, wenn ihr einig seid und treu." (Never will the Empire be destroyed, so long as you are united and loyal.)

During World War II, an American shell damaged the statue beyond repair. After the division of Germany in 1949, the first President of the Federal Republic of Germany, Theodor Heuss, turned the corner into a monument to German unity. He installed the coats of arms of all German states (Länder) and former territories. A huge German flag replaced the statue.

With the fall of the wall and reunification, three sections of the wall were installed at the monument. A year later, emblems of the new federal states were added. After considerable discussion about what should stand on the corner, Werner and Anneliese Theisen of Koblenz offered to bear the cost of reconstruction of the former equestrian statue. On 25 September 1993, the new statue was inaugurated. Today, a large national flag and those of sixteen states fly at the corner. The three sections of wall are now dedicated to the "victims of the separation." What we saw from the Ehrenbreitstein fortress was the huge flag that flew at the corner.

By the time we got down to shoreline, it was time for dinner. Almost directly below the fortress is Diehl's Hotel. Their restaurant, the Clemens, overlooked the Rhein and with the sun setting across the river, it was a magnificent sight. Through the picture window next to our table we could see the corner, the basilica of St Kastor, the Palace of Koblenz, the old town and the departure piers of various sightseeing ships.

After a typical German meal of schnitzel and fried potatoes, we crossed back to Koblenz. We had seen a carnival of sorts near the corner, so we decided to investigate. To our delight, there was a small festival going on, so we found a table and ordered some Rhein wine. Alas, the waitress misunderstood and brought a Mosel. We could tell by the color of the bottle. The color of the tall, slender bottles tells you what region the wine comes from. Brown bottles come from the Rhine region. Green bottles come from the Mosel area or from Alsace. The shape is used elsewhere around the world for wines made from grape varieties associated with Germany—like Riesling and Gewürztraminer. We didn't make a fuss and drank the fine white wine in no time. Another couple from the group joined us, so this time we ordered two bottles of wine. And so it went for quite some time. The six of us sat there enjoying the cool evening, the Rhein itself, and some of the finest wines in Germany. We did notice, however, that as our consumption increased, the quality of the wine we purchased decreased.

Fortunately, as residents of West Germany, we had studied their wines extensively. As a matter of fact, Edie and I joined the Pieroth Winery in West Berlin. As members, we were required to purchase at least one case every month. For our loyalty, the winery invited us to special tastings periodically throughout the year where we learned to decipher the confounding German wine labels. We also got to taste some incredibly fine wines.

If the reader will indulge me, I'll present a quick tutorial on reading German wine labels. The Germans instituted a quality rating system. In that system, the highest quality wines are labeled QmP (Qualitätswein mit Prädikat), meaning "quality wine with distinction." QmP wines are categorized by the ripeness of the grapes at harvest. It is difficult for German grapes to ripen, because the vineyards are so far north. For this reason, grape sugars are highly prized. The highest sugar content and potential alcohol content occur in the ripest grapes. German wines are categorized from the least ripe to the ripest as follows:

- Kabinett
- Spätlese
- Auslese
- Beerenauslese
- Trockenbeerenauslese
- Eiswein

Remember that these terms have nothing to do with the quality of the wine. They merely identify the ripeness of the grape at harvest. If the bottle has the QmP designation, or Qualitätswein mit Prädikat, you know it is a quality wine. What many Americans don't know is at the Kabinett, Spatlese, and Auslese levels, the grapes can be fermented to produce a completely dry wine. So, if searching for a dry wine, look for the word Kabinett on the label. Other terms to look for are "Trocken" (German for dry), "Classic," or "Selection." At the highest ripeness levels, the grapes have so much sugar at harvest that the wines almost can't help but be sweet.

Although there are a number of fine dry wines, Germany's sweet wines have achieved the most international acclaim. The most notable are Trockenbeerenauslese wines made from grapes affected by the noble rot, Botrytis cinerea; the late harvest Beerenauslese wines, which may or may not have been affected by Bortrytis, and the thick, intensely sweet ice wines, made from frozen grapes or Eiswein. The Reisling is Germany's signature grape, which was our preference that evening.

The less ripe grapes produce a less costly bottle. We spent the remainder of the evening imbibing in Kabinett after Kabinett. When we finished, we were surprised to learn we had consumed some fifty bottles. That accounted for our inability to negotiate curbs, etc. From the outdoor wine café, we meandered to the carnival. Our bacchanalia concluded, and our money running short, we decided to attend the fest. We could hear and see it in the distance and our curiosity was peaked. As we drew closer, the familiar sights, sounds, and aromas captivated us. We were ready to enjoy an hour or two before heading back to the hotel, and rest for our return trip down river.

The ride that immediately caught our collective eye was one that we'd all enjoyed in our youth at one fair or another, bumper cars! We couldn't wait to crash head on into one another, possibly shaking off the effects of the wine, pun intended.

We purchased our tickets and gleefully ran to our cars. The ride was exactly the same as those I'd ridden on in my youth at carnivals. We waited anxiously for the electricity to be turned on and the ride to begin. Eventually, the operator threw the switch and our vehicles came to life. Each of us barreled toward the other hoping to knock a filling or two loose. Crash! Bam! Crunch! Mission accomplished. We made a beeline for the other cars on the floor with as much speed as we could muster. We six Americans, in three bumper cars were on a mission to make contact with as many other cars as time allowed. As we plowed into other cars, we roared with exaltation at having accomplished our goal. We expected our German counterparts to react with similar joy. Instead, they glared at us and began to shout their disapproval. I immediately pulled close to Danny who spoke fluent German and screamed, "What's happening?" He looked and listened for a long second and responded, "They want us to go around in a line and not bump into each other! They're mad as hell that we're willfully crashing into them."

What! I couldn't believe it! They really wanted us to join in a leisurely ride around the edge of the bumper car floor. I wondered why they even called them bumper cars. While I was pondering the inanity of the situation, I managed to have a head on crash with an elderly German couple. That was the final straw for the operator. He shut the ride down, came out on the floor, and motioned us off the ride. We were being thrown off a bumper car ride for "bumping" into other cars. Incredible! The operator was not nice about the eviction. Again, according to Danny's translation, we were not nor would we ever be welcome at this fest again. Of special note is the fact that our annual Berlin American Volksfest had a bumper car ride where Americans and Berliners purposefully crashed one another's vehicles. When we got off, we watched to see what was acceptable. Remarkably, the riders got into a neat, orderly line front bumper to rear and drove in a circle. No crashes! No bumps! I want to say, "No fun." But, I would be wrong. The Germans were having a wonderful time driving in a controlled circle. They waved at each other, smiled, and shouted greetings and good wishes. I chuckled. We had made the mistake of thinking what Americans did must be done by everyone. We should have watched for a while before we got on the ride. To this day, I've not met anyone else who had been evicted from a bumper car ride for bumping cars.

We made our way back to the hotel and prepared for the next day's return trip. The next morning was uneventful, except for an incredible headache. We had a couple glasses of wine and caught our boat headed down river to Rüdesheim where we would spend the night at the Hotel Lindenwirt. Edie and I relaxed for this leg of the journey. We didn't take photos or explore the ship. We sat on the foredeck in comfortable lounges and watched the Rhein go by. I remember Edie being especially intrigued by those who lived in their boats on the water, ferrying cargo up and down the river. The sight of children playing and laundry drying on passing ships fascinated her.

We docked in Rüdesheim early in the afternoon. Once again, I had to make sure of our reservations and room assignments. I was happy to see that we hadn't left anyone in Koblenz. I was happier to see Lowell upright as he took his room key from me.

Hotel Lindenwirt is a nice traditional hotel, partly built inside an old and romantic medieval town gate. It was quaint, historic, and rested on the fabled Drosselgasse. The lane is barely three meters wide and about 144 meters long. Along the cobbled street, one can find numerous wine cellars, hotels, and restaurants. Some three million visitors walk the lane annually.

After getting everyone checked in successfully, Edie and I decided to visit the Niederwald Monument. In another rare display of courage, Edie agreed to take the cable car to the high ridge above Rüdesheim. Her courage was rewarded by the view of the Rhein gorge that unfolded before us as we rose higher and higher above the vineyards that lay mere meters below our feet. The Niederwald was impressive to say the least. On September 16th, none other than Wilhelm I laid the first stone. Constructed to commemorate the foundation of the German Empire after the end of Franco-Prussian War, it wasn't completed and dedicated until 1883. At thirty-eight meters tall, it represents the union of all Germans. Did I mention it was enormous? The central figure is the Germania monument. Standing 10.5 meters, she holds the recovered crown of the emperor in her right hand and in her left the Imperial Sword. On a relief beneath her, Emperor Wilhelm I rides a horse with his nobility, army commanders, and soldiers. Engrave on the relief are the lyrics to Wacht am Rhein (Watch on the Rhine). The peace statue rests on her left with the war statue on her right. As remarkable as the monument was, the view from her base was even more so. It was worth the trip.

Upon our return to terra firma, we joined the group on the balcony of our hotel directly above the Drosselgasse. Edie and I were introduced formally to the mother of one of my flight colleagues. According to her, she read palms. Judging from her supposed accuracy, she'd been thoroughly briefed by her son. Most Catholics, practicing or not, are intrigued by anything "spiritual." As an ardent non-practitioner at that time, I agreed to letting her delve into my shadowy past and present. Typically, her generalities would have been true for the majority of the men on the trip. Others were amazed, I was amused.

Fresh from our brush with the Twilight Zone, we ate, visited a wine cellar or two, and turned in. Since we had some time to kill on the final full day of our break, Edie, Annette, Danny and I decided to explore the Alderturm (Eagle Tower). It is the corner tower of the old city walls constructed during the 15th century. It is 20.5 meters high or approximately four stories. It has a spiral interior staircase against the meter thick wall. The stairs are dank, medieval, dark, claustrophobic and simply wonderful. On each floor, we were greeted by medieval suits of armor, weaponry, cooking utensils, and other period paraphernalia. The tower included a dungeon that was accessible only through a hole at the top of the cellar. In centuries past, the tower was located directly on the banks of the Rhein. It was from this tower that townspeople signaled breakup of ice floes here that a pole with a flaming basket was mounted to signal the breakup of the ice floes. During the last century, the tower housed an inn called "Zum Adler" (To The Eagle), from which the tower takes its name. Johann Wolfgang von Goethe was a guest here several times during his visits to Ruedesheim. Today, the Adlerturm is owned by a bank.

After the tower, we had a couple of hours left before our train departed, so we decided to tour the Asbach Uralt Distillery. One of the finest brandies in the world, Asbach Uralt, has been made here since 1892. The tour was free, the tasting room was historic, and the brandy, delicious. We only bought one bottle, but the visit was incredible.

By then, time was running out to catch our train. We made it to the train station with a few minutes to spare. Danny suggested we get some wine, cheese and bread for the trip to Frankfurt and the duty train back to West Berlin. After counting our combined cash, we barely had enough for some inexpensive wine (Kabinett), a pound of cheese and a fresh loaf of bread. The final concern I had was the train. I had contracted to have a car added just for our group. As the train pulled into the station, I was more than relieved to see a sign on the side of the trailing car that read simply, "Jones." We scrambled aboard, settled in and began to share our dinner. The trip to Frankfurt and West Berlin was uneventful. No one had enough energy left to do anything but sleep. One day, Edie and I plan on taking another boat trip down the beautiful Rhein.

A PIECE OF THE WALL

It was a glorious evening, one of those you dream about. A light breeze gently pushed fifty-degree air through leaves highlighted by a full harvest moon. I had just finished an especially exhilarating and rewarding "swing shift" at our Teufelsberg site. To celebrate, a couple of coworkers and I decided to go to one of the local watering holes for "just one." We boarded a blue Air Force Mercedes bus and got off at the first U-Bahn stop we could find. As we purchased our tickets, we could hear and feel the rumble of subterranean trains arriving and departing deep below.

Our destination was a Bierstube that was a familiar stop on Podbielskialle. As we entered, we ordered our usual. I requested a liter of Doppelbock in a cold Stein, while Reptile and Animal, participants in several misadventures herein chronicled, ordered Jägermeister with an Apfelkorn chaser. After our first long draught, we began to talk about nothing in particular. Eventually, as usual, conversation drifted to the ever-present wall.

West Berlin was an island; the very existence of the Berlin Wall made it so. Everyone knew its history, and virtually no one could escape its presence. Reptile wondered, "How much of the original wall is left?" I replied that I didn't think there was any left other that what was visible at Bernauer Strasse.

Animal immediately interjected that the French Sector still had entire sections of the original wall standing. Unfortunately, a concrete covering had been applied on the West side while the original brick and stone facade was visible only in the East. Reptile sighed as he ordered another round, "So, getting a piece of the original is out of the question." Animal's reply marked the beginning of our adventure, "I'm not sure. I don't know that we couldn't get a piece or two of the original if we really wanted it."

"Are you nuts?" Reptile taunted, and so they were off. "Just one" became two, then three, as they argued over several "fool proof" plans for securing these rarest of souvenirs. Oddly enough, one can buy dozens on eBay today. They reasoned, inaccurately, that the ubiquitous guard towers were indeed farther apart in the French Sector, in that it was wooded and sparsely populated. It would be easier to get over the wall, hack a piece or two off, and get back before being captured or shot. Eventually, Reptile said he knew a spot on the Havel River past Tegel Airport where the towers were more than a quarter mile apart. Laughingly, he offered, "Heck, the guards don't expect to see someone trying to get into East Berlin. They're trained to look for people trying to escape. That would buy one of us precious time to get over the wall unnoticed, if he was lucky. Hell, I bet the VOPOs (Volkspolizei) wouldn't even shoot. If one of us went over dead center between two towers"—he was now unstoppable—"it will be too far for a good shot. They'd probably try to close the gap on their motorcycles first."

Although he sounded convincing, neither Animal nor I thought it possible. Even so, we continued to plan the break-in. I offered that a simple length of rope wrapped once around the waist and through the intruder's belt loops, manned at each end by an accomplice ready to pull hard at a moment's notice, would allow quick entry and escape. Animal thought a simple hammer and chisel would complete our tool kit. Whatever was hacked off could be tossed over the wall before the intruder climbed back and before he was apprehended or worse.

With the plan complete, we finished our drinks and decided to go home. The game had been fun, but carrying it though to fruition was unanimously considered lunacy. Somewhere in our planning we had discussed all that could go wrong. There we too many ways for one of us to end up sporting a toe tag, if the East Germans even used such an item.

Resigned to abandoning the idea, we caught a bus heading in the general direction of home. As luck or fate would have it, another flight member, Sandy, got on a couple of stops later. Tall and attractive, she had been out with one of her many suitors. Greeting Reptile and Animal, she sat next to me and began to chat. In the course of our conversation, Animal blurted out our invasion plan. At first she laughed, stating that suicide might be less lethal. However, after a long moment of reflection, a smile began to form and she had to admit that she wouldn't mind having a piece of the original Berlin Wall. A challenge, even as half-hearted as this one was, had been given. I noticed the look of determination growing on Reptile and Animal's faces and knew we would try it. Sandy bid us good night and got off at the next stop. Animal, Reptile, and I began to talk in earnest. We made our way to Animal's apartment where remarkably we discovered everything we needed for the escapade. The game was afoot.

After another hour, we found ourselves in a remote section of the French Sector. We tiptoed for another fifteen or so minutes before we caught sight of the wall; the very spot Reptile had described earlier. There was no discussion about who would go over. I had only consumed Bier and was the nearest to sober—I also weighed much less than my partners. Carefully, we laced the rope through five belt loops and around my waist. After testing it for strength, it was time to give our plan one good attempt. As I scrambled for all I was worth, Reptile and Animal hoisted me atop the infamous wall. We were in luck. A band of ominously dark clouds obscured the moon and seemed to fade the floodlights shining on "no-man's land," a death strip tens of meters wide that were filled with mines and/or attack dogs. The strip provided border guards with a clear shot at anyone who tried to escape to the West. With effort, I could make out the guards in the distant towers to my right and left. They seemed so far away and, as predicted, appeared preoccupied with the East rather than the wall. The Wall! It stretched like a ribbon into the distance on one side and, after a half-kilometer or so, disappeared into the blue-black waters of the Havel on the other. At my back, deep woods obscured the West while in front of me was an endless stretch of barren terrain pockmarked with barbed wire, bunkers, and towers—stark witnesses to the tale of life in the East.

I managed to avoid the shards of glass and metal imbedded atop the wall and lowered myself cautiously into the East, all the while questioning Reptile's mastery of ballistics. I must admit that the thought of dogs and landmines came to me only after I had touched down. Also, it was only then that I remembered I was still in my fatigues. I paused for a moment to allow a flood of adrenaline to run its course. I wasn't scared—that surprised me. I actually felt a sense of exhilaration and accomplishment. I took time to take in an awesome sight few had seen and even fewer had enjoyed.

After a long minute, it was time to get down to business. Inspecting the wall with my hands as well as my eyes, I was gratified to find many fissures and crevices into which the chisel fit. I chose one I knew would yield a large chunk and inserted the business end of the tool deep into the wall. Retrieving the hammer from my belt, I took a deep breath, raised the hammer high, and let the blunt end fall heavily onto the chisel. The shrill, metal-on-metal sound startled me as it shattered the silence. Through the wall, I heard Reptile and Animal utter muffled curses. A tower searchlight immediately began to rake the barren strip behind me as I increased my pace, knowing it would only be a matter of seconds before the lights found their target. Another deafening blow, then another, as piece after fabled piece dropped to my feet. A flurry of activity at the guard tower to my left alerted me to men rushing to their motorcycles. Engines roared to life as I frantically threw pieces as far over the wall. It dawned on me that if I hit either Reptile or Animal, I might as well toss up my hands and surrender. Inevitably, a spotlight as bright as any I had ever seen found me and fixed on my location. More shouts and the unmistakable sound of a bolt slamming home announced the time for my hasty departure. Tugging frantically for all I was worth, I screamed for my comrades to pull me over. The rope went taut as I frantically clawed my way back up the wall. Hands and knees bleeding from ill-repaired mortar and brick not to mention the shards of glass and nails imbedded on top, I leaped as far as I could as the first motorcycle began to downshift.

"Quiet!" ordered Reptile. "Shut the @#% up and hug the wall!"

I was in no condition to hug anything, so I just lay there bleeding, desperately trying to catch my breath. I'm certain I didn't look nearly as adventurous as I had, just minutes earlier. We could hear the VOPOs on the other side frantically trying to determine what had just happened. We knew enough of their modus operandi to know that none of them would top the wall for fear of having a comrade-in-arms suddenly become executioner. A couple of eternities passed before we heard the motorcycle engines fade in the distance. We understood enough German to know that they had no clue to what had happened or why. We also knew they would not run the risk of taking this any further. They were more than reluctant to look like fools in front of the Stasi, let alone the Soviets and the KGB.

Strangely sober, we waited a long while for normal breathing to resume. Animal pulled out a flashlight and got up.

I heard myself shout, "Don't turn that thing on! I've had just about enough light for tonight."

We set about on all fours trying to find the pieces I had hacked from the other side. Eventually, we found seven large fragments, two of which are still in my possession. Elated and relieved, we made our way back to the bus stop. Slapping each other on the back again and again displaying emotion know only those who've "dodged a bullet," we boarded, divvied up our precious booty, and went home. Sleep came rapidly and easily.

I remember it being a bit of a chore trying to explain to my wife how I got pieces of the original wall. This was pre-conversion to following the Savior, and I had no problem stretching the truth to keep harmony in the home. I believe my story fell apart when she began to inquire about my many small abrasions and cuts. Eventually, she did get the story out of me. To my surprise, her look of resignation coupled with a small dose of incredulity was her only reaction. To this day, although we've told friends the tale, we rarely discuss it with each other.

The next evening at work, the flight was all abuzz about our nocturnal exploits. Animal was not known for his reserve. He had told everyone except the flight commander who would be kept in the dark on the chance he would report us for the numerous statutes and international laws we had broken, not to mention the impact it might have on our security clearances. When Reptile and I arrived, we were met with applause. Reptile quietly took in the adulation while Animal lapped it up, reveling in the moment. When all had gone back to work, I found my way to Sandy's workstation. Reaching into my pocket, I removed a crude piece of brick. Gently, almost reverently, laying it on the desk in front of her typewriter, I smiled and walked away.

EPILOGUE

Sunday, November 9, 1989 was a pleasant fall day in San Angelo. Normally, I would have occupied myself with the recently opened Texas deer season, but I was more concerned with moving my wife and son to Denton. I had retired in September after twenty-three years in the USAF. Five weeks into my job as the public relations manager for the local blood service, the now merged GTE hired me as a management educator. I had already moved to start the job with my family remaining behind to sell the house. Further, we would be leaving our daughter with dear friends so that she could continue her education at Angelo State University. The house, to say the least, was in turmoil and our minds were otherwise occupied when I heard in both English and German, "The Berlin Wall is falling! Die Berliner Mauer fällt!"

I must admit I didn't catch the initial announcement and still to this day don't know what channel we were watching. It was the subsequent reporting and the riveting pictures of the all-too-familiar Brandenburg Gate area that captured my attention. I called Edie into the living room to see the unbelievable sight. People had mobbed the wall and even climbed atop the dreadful edifice. Amazingly, some were pounding away with sledge hammers ignoring a haphazard attempt by border guards to stop them with fire hoses.

We couldn't believe our eyes. After I threw a glance at Edie, my eyes darted to the shelf that held the pieces of wall I'd risked so much to get. Now, dozens if not hundreds of delirious Berliners were happily knocking chunk after chunk into the air without any attempt to recover the souvenirs.

I must admit I hadn't followed events in Eastern Europe as closely as I had mere months earlier when I taught World Affairs at our NCO Academy; however, a brief review of those events makes that year far more memorable than just the year I retired and reentered the civilian world. Countries that might as well have been on different planets even though only a short automobile trip apart suddenly experienced political movement that swept like wildfire throughout the East. The list is impressive and shows the power of freedom once tasted and savored. The juggernaut could not be stopped; it was like trying to put the proverbial genie back in the bottle.

- Poland (April 5): The Communist government and Solidarity (Polish: Solidarność[1]) agree to share power and hold free elections.
- Yugoslavia (May 8): The nationalist Slobodan Milosevic is elected as president.
- Poland (June 4): Solidarity wins a huge majority of the vote, including ninety-six of one hundred Senate seats.
- Poland (August 19): Mazowiecki is elected as Poland's first non-Communist prime minister.
- Hungary (September 10): Sixty thousand East Germans transit Hungary to cross into Austria.
- Yugoslavia (September 27): Slovenia asserts its right to secede from Yugoslavia.
- Hungary (October 7): The formerly communist Socialist Workers Party renounces Marxism and embraces democratic socialism. It is renamed the Hungarian Socialist Party.
- East Germany (October 18): Mass demonstrations force President Eric Honecker to resign.
- Hungary (October 18): Parliament ends the one-party monopoly and announces elections would be held in 1990.
- East Germany (November 9): The Berlin Wall is opened and five million people come to Berlin to celebrate the end of the wall, the end of the Cold War, the end of Communism, and the reunification of Germany.

- Bulgaria (November 10): Todor Zhikov, head of state and leader of the Communist Party for thirty-five years, resigns.
- Czechoslovakia (November 17): Encouraged by recent events in East Germany, hundreds of thousands of protesters march in Prague.
- Czechoslovakia (December 10): President Gustav Husak resigns and installs a coalition cabinet with communists in the minority.
- Bulgaria (December 13): The Communist Party renounces their monopoly on power.
- Romania (December 18): Regular military forces, police, and Securitate (secret police of Communist Romania) fire on thousands of demonstrators, hundreds are killed and buried in mass graves. As Christmas arrives, everyone in Europe watches the revolution on television.
- Romania (December 22): The army revolts and joins the demonstrators it fired upon a week earlier. The National Salvation Front declares the government to be overthrown.
- Romania (December 25): In a two-hour trial, the Communist dictator Nicolae Ceausescu and his wife Elena are convicted of genocide and immediately executed by machine gunfire.
- Poland (December 26): The new government announces radical free-market reform plan.
- Czechoslovakia (December 29): While leader of the Civic Forum, playwright and human rights campaigner Vaclav Havel, becomes president by a unanimous vote of the Federal Assembly.

A chain of events was set in motion that would bring the end of the "Evil Empire" itself. At 12:01 a.m. on October 3, 1990, the

German Democratic Republic ceased to exist, and in December 1991, the Soviet Union was no more.

Standing in front of our TV, we had no way of knowing that both East Germany and the Soviet Union would topple so soon. I had always believed their demise was inevitable but hadn't given much thought as to when. We were too enthralled with current events in our former home. It was then that Edie turned to me and said softly, "Ed, you won!" She must have seen the quizzical look on my face because she uttered the phrase again and then explained that those of us who had "fought" the Cold War against Communist Europe had finally prevailed. All the treasure spent and all the lives lost had not been in vain—the West had indeed won and I had been a part of it. We both began to cry and didn't stop for quite some time. To this day, the thought of that moment still brings tears.

It's been more than two decades since the wall fell and over three decades since last we trod the streets of West Berlin, but the memories of that place and the feelings they engender are as fresh as the faces of our beloved grandchildren. We hope to return some day, but if we don't, we're thankful that we lived there at such an incredible time.

ENDNOTES

1. Komitet Gosudarstvennoj Bezopastnosti (Committee for State Security), which was the official name of the umbrella organization that served as the Soviet Union's premier security agency, secret police, and intelligence agency, from 1954 to 1991.

2. DLIFLC is a United States Department of Defense(DoD) educational and research institution, which provides linguistic and cultural instruction to the department of defense, other federal agencies and numerous and varied other customers. The Defense Language Institute is responsible for the Defense Language Program, and the bulk of the Defense Language Institute's activities involve educating DoD members in assigned languages. Other functions include planning, curriculum development, and research in second-language acquisition.

3. Sergei Mikhailovich Eisenstein (January 23, 1898–February 11, 1948) was a revolutionary Soviet Russian film director and film theorist noted in particular for his silent films *Strike, Battleship Potemkin and October*, as well as historical epics, *Alexander Nevsky and Ivan the Terrible*. His work vastly influenced early film makers owing to his innovative use of and writings about montage.

4. The National Cryptologic School (NCS) is a Cryptologic Training School within the National Security Agency (NSA). It is responsible for designing, developing, and delivering curriculum Cryptology, Information Assurance, Language, and Leadership. NCS courses are provided to

the civilian and military population of NSA, as well as the Intelligence Community, the military services, and the Central Security Service (CSS).

TROIKA

1. In November 1945, the Western powers proposed, and Marshall of the Soviet Union Zhukov agreed to, three 20 mile-wide air corridors connecting Berlin with Hamburg, Frankfurt/Main, and Hannover-Bueckeburg. From this came a set of flight rules published by the Allied Control Authority Air Directorate on October 22, 1946, which proved to be crucial. The rules not only further defined the air corridors, but also established the Berlin Control Zone which permitted airplanes landing and taking off from Berlin airfields to fly within a twenty-mile radius of Berlin. This permitted Allied aircraft to overfly the Soviet Sector of Berlin and the Soviet Zone on their approaches and departures. The three air corridors were formally specified as Frankfurt-Berlin, Bueckeburg-Berlin, and Hamburg-Berlin, each twenty English miles wide. The agreement did not specify altitude, but by practice and custom Allied aircraft have been constrained by a ten thousand foot ceiling although the right to fly higher had never been yielded in principle.

2. The Weimar Republic was the democratic and republican period of Germany from 1919 to 1933. The republic grew out of German Revolution that followed World War I. A national assembly convened in Weimar in 1919. There, a new constitution for the German Reich was written. The

rise to power of the Nazi Party and Adolf Hitler in 1933 ended the attempt at a liberal democracy.

3   Speer was Hitler's chief architect before becoming his Minister for Armaments during the war.

4   Tempelhof Airport closed all operations on October 30, 2008, despite the efforts of numerous protesters to prevent the closure.

5   The Bundeswehr, German for "Federal Defense Force"; is the name of the unified armed forces of the Federal Republic of Germany and their civil administration and procurement authorities.

6   Radar intelligence is a specialized form of ELINT (electronic intelligence), which categorizes and locates the target's radar emissions.

7   SIGINT is intelligence gathering by intercepting signals between people (COMINT or communications intelligence) or machines (ELINT or electronic intelligence), or mixtures of the two. Since sensitive information is often encrypted, signals intelligence often involves the use of cryptanalysis or code breaking. However, even when the messages themselves cannot be decrypted, traffic analysis or the study of who is communicating with whom and in what quantity can often produce valuable information.

8   "Greenwood'" is both a forest on the east side of the Havel and a locality of the borough of Charlottenburg-Wilmersdorf. While the name derives from the Grunewald hunting lodge of 1543, the neighborhood developed out of a so-called "mansion colony" at the western end of the Kurfürstendamm. Its beauty caused Otto von Bismark to advertise it as an ideal location for the upper class of Berlin from 1880 on. Today, the social structure of Grunewald

is still influenced by these origins. The Rot-Weiss Tennis Club, home of the WTA Tour German Open, has been located in the district since 1897.

9 ECHELON is a name used in global media and in popular culture to describe a SIGINT collection and analysis network operated on behalf of the five signatory states to the UK-USA Security Agreement (Australia, Canada, New Zealand, the United Kingdom, and the United States.) ECHELON was created to monitor the military and diplomatic communications of the Soviet Union and its Eastern Bloc allies during the Cold War in the early 1960s, but since the end of the Cold War it is believed to search also for hints of terrorist plots, drug dealer's plans, and political and diplomatic intelligence.

A PAIR OF SHORTS AND A LONG

1 The "Iron Curtain" was the boundary which symbolically, ideologically, and physically divided Europe into two separate areas from the end of World War II until the end of the Cold War, roughly 1945 to 1991. The first recorded use of the term was in 1920 by Ethel Snowden in her book Through Bolshevik Russia. German politician and Nazi Minister of Propaganda Joseph Goebbels was the first to refer to an "Iron Curtain" coming down across Europe after World War II, in a manifesto he published in the German newspaper Das Reich in February 1945. The term was not widely used until March 5, 1946, when it was popularized by Winston Churchill in his "Sinews of Peace" address.

2   The U.S. Army Garrison based in West Berlin from 1945 to 1994. It included all United States forces stationed in West Berlin during the Cold War.

3   Fragging is a term from the Vietnam War, used primarily by U.S. military personnel, most commonly meaning to assassinate an unpopular officer of one's own fighting unit, often by means of a fragmentation grenade. A hand grenade was often used because it would not leave any fingerprints, and because a ballistics test could not be done. A fragging victim could also be killed by intentional friendly fire during combat. In either case, the death would be blamed on the enemy, and, due to the dead man's unpopularity, the perpetrator could assume that no one would contradict the story.

4   Three of the numerous beers served in Berlin.

5   The official Secret Police of East Germany.

6   The Wannsee Conference was a meeting of senior officials of the Nazi German regime, held in the Berlin suburb of Wannsee on 20 January 1942. The purpose of the conference was to inform administrative heads of Departments responsible for various policies relating to Jews, that Reinhard Heydrich had been appointed as the chief executor of the "Final solution to the Jewish question", and to obtain their full support. In the course of the meeting, Heydrich presented a plan, presumably approved by Hitler, for the deportation of the Jewish population of Europe to German-occupied areas in eastern Europe, and the use of the Jews fit for labor on road-building projects, in the course of which they would eventually die, the surviving remnant to be annihilated after completion of the projects. The plan was never carried out as conceived, as it was predicated on the continued occupation of Polish and Soviet

lands then under German control. Instead, as Soviet forces gradually pushed back the German lines, most of the Jews of German-occupied Europe were sent to extermination or concentration camps, or killed where they lived.

7   Burgee: A small flag with the insignia of the yacht club it represents. It distinguishes members and boats of one club from another.

8   Mushy peas are dried marrowfat peas, which are first soaked overnight in water and bicarbonate of soda and then simmered with a little sugar and salt until they form a thick green lumpy soup. Sometimes mint is used to alter the flavor. Green coloring is often used.

9   Bangers are a type of sausage common to the UK. They get their name from the sausage's predilection toward bursting or "banging" open during high frying temperatures. In fact, to avoid losing some of the sausage, bangers may be boiled first, and sliced lengthwise prior to frying or grilling. They are white in appearance, and are composed primarily of pork butt, a small amount of breadcrumbs, and water. They are normally pleasantly spiced with both sweet and savory spices. The average banger will have both salt and pepper, as well as sage, ginger and mace or allspice. Spices differ depending upon the brand.

WE CALL HIM PRINCE JIM

1   Office of Special Investigations

2   U.S. Army Criminal Investigative Command

PERSPECTIVE

1. "Our Marxists declare that the capitalist system of world economy conceals elements of crisis and war, that the development of world capitalism does not follow a steady and even course forward, but proceeds through crises and catastrophes. The uneven development of the capitalist countries leads in time to sharp disturbances in their relations, and the group of countries which consider themselves inadequately provided with raw materials and export markets try usually to change this situation and to change the position in their favor by means of armed force. As a result of these factors, the capitalist world is sent into two hostile camps and war follows."

2. Under this federal program, Truman ordered the Justice Department to produce a list of possible subversives. Further, it established loyalty boards, established lists of dissident organizations, and authorized the dismissal of people considered to be "bad" security risks.

3. The Treaty of Brussels signed between Belgium, France, Luxembourg, the Netherlands and the United Kingdom, as an expansion to the preceding year's defense pledge, the Dunkirk Treaty signed between Britain and France. As the Treaty of Brussels contained a mutual defense clause, it provided a basis which the 1954 Paris Conference established the Western European Union (weU) upon.

4. After brilliant offensives in Korea and the capture of Pyonyang it appeared the Korean war was finished, but the Chinese attacked the UN Forces, crossing the Yalu river with Four infantry armies, three artillery divisions, an anti-aircraft regiment and two hundred sixty thousand

men. The UN forces were forced to retreat and a standoff was achieved at the 38th parallel.

During a lull in the fighting, the U.S. announced that negotiations might be possible with both sides separated by the 38th parallel. As usual, MacArthur rejected the idea of a negotiated settlement. MacArthur continued to make statements that were contrary to the official position of Washington, and specifically Truman. The arrogant MacArthur had derailed the U.S. initiative by daring China to continue the war. The Pentagon received his message, which infuriated many high ranking officials. Acheson said that MacArthur had "shot his mouth off" for the last time. The next morning Truman awakened to the news of MacArthur's "sabotage". At that moment he could no longer tolerate his insubordination. Truman had considered firing MacArthur many times previous to this, but this was the last straw. Actually the order of Dec. 6 which MacArthur had disobeyed was explicit enough to warrant court-martial proceedings. MacArthur's statements were causing consternation in Washington as was his insulting personal letter to Ridgway. His advice letter to the House of Representatives again infuriated everyone. The British Government called the letter the "most dangerous" of an "apparently unending series of indiscretions." They claimed it was another irresponsible statement without the authorization of the U.S. or any U.N. member government. The Foreign Secretary complained that MacArthur wanted a war with China, and his leadership could no longer be tolerated. In reality, MacArthur did want to invade China, but in a dangerous way. He suggested using nuclear weapons against them if he was allowed to invade. On Apr. 6 a meeting was held with Truman to determine how to get rid of MacArthur. Truman insisted "I'm going to fire him right now." MacArthur was ordered to turnover his command at once to Lt. General Ridgway. General Bradley warned Truman that if MacArthur heard about the orders before they reached him officially, he might resign with an arrogant flair. Truman exclaimed "He isn't going to resign on me, I want him fired". MacArthur's dismissal was announced on late night radio:

"With deep regret I have concluded that General of the Army Douglas MacArthur is unable to give his wholehearted support to the policies of the U.S. Government and of the U.N. in matters pertaining to his official duties. In view of the specific responsibilities imposed upon me by the Constitution of the U.S. and the added responsibilities entrusted to me by the U.N. I have decided that I must make a change in command in the Far East. I have, therefore, relieved General MacArthur of his command and have designated Lt. Gen. Matthew Ridgway as his successor." MacArthur accepted the unsurprising news impassively. He said that he had never disobeyed orders, and that his dismissal was a plot in Washington to weaken the American position in the Far East.

5   The 17th parallel division between North and South Vietnam was the result of a Chinese proposal at the Geneva Conference of 1954 which ended the French war in Vietnam. China did not want a strong, unified Vietnam on its southern border and easily convinced the great powers to go along with their proposal. Ho Chi Minh was virtually helpless. He had won the war but lost the peace. He did obtain the promise of an election to reunify Vietnam which he was confident he could win. President Eisenhower saw to it that the election never took place.

6   The Poznań 1956 protests, also known as Poznań 1956 uprising or Poznań June (Polish: Poznański Czerwiec),

were the first of several massive protests against the communist government of the People's Republic of Poland. Demonstrations by workers demanding better conditions began on June 28, 1956, at Poznań's Cegielski Factories and were met with violent repression.

A crowd of approximately one hundred thousand gathered in the city center near the UB secret police building. Four hundred tanks and ten thousand soldiers of Ludowe Wojsko Polskie and the Internal Security Corps under Polish-Soviet general Stanislav Poplavsky were ordered to suppress the demonstration and during the pacification fired at the protesting civilians. The death toll was placed between 57 and 78 people including a thirteen-year-old boy, Romek Strzałkowski. Hundreds of people sustained injuries. Nonetheless the Poznań protests were an important milestone on the way to the installation of a less Soviet-controlled government in Poland in October.

[7] The Kitchen Debate was a series of impromptu exchanges between then U.S. Vice President Richard Nixon and Soviet Premier Nikita Khrushchev at the opening of the American National Exhibition at Sokolniki Park in Moscow on July 24, 1959. For the exhibition, an entire house was built that the American exhibitors claimed anyone in America could afford. It was filled with labor-saving and recreational devices meant to represent the fruits of the capitalist American consumer market. Both men argued for their country's industrial accomplishments, with Khrushchev stressing the Soviets' focus on "things that matter" rather than luxury. He satirically asked if there was a machine that "puts food into the mouth and pushes it down". Nixon responded by saying at least the competition was technological, rather than military.

8. Perhaps the most famous spy swap involved Francis Gary Powers, a U.S. pilot who had been shot down in a U-2 spy plane over the Soviet Union in 1960. Two years later, Powers was traded for Rudolf Abel, the leading figure in the famous "Hollow Nickel" case that began when a newsboy discovered a tiny message hidden inside a coin. Abel had posed for years as a photographer in Brooklyn before his arrest in 1957. The two men were brought to separate sides of the Glienicker Brücke (bridge), which connects East and West Berlin across Lake Wannsee. As the spies waited, negotiators talked in the center of the bridge where a white line divided East from West. Finally, Powers and Abel were waved forward and crossed the border into freedom at the same moment—8:52 a.m., Berlin time. Just before their transfer, Frederic Pryor—an American student held by East German authorities since August 1961—was released to American authorities at another border checkpoint.

9. In matters concerning information security, whether public or private sector, compartmentalization is the limiting of access to information to persons or other entities that have a need to know it in order to perform certain tasks. The concept originated in the handling of classified information in military and intelligence applications. The basis for compartmentalization was the idea that, if fewer people know the details of a mission or task, the risk or likelihood that such information could be compromised or fall into the hands of the opposition is decreased. Hence, varying levels of clearance within organizations exist. Yet, even if someone has the highest clearance, certain "compartmentalized" information, identified by code words referring to particular types of secret information, may still be restricted to certain operators, even with a lower overall security clearance. Information marked this way is said to be code word—classified. One famous example of this was the ultra

secret, where documents were marked "Top Secret Ultra": "Top Secret" marked its security level, and the "Ultra" keyword further restricted its readership to only those cleared to read "Ultra" documents.

10 The Bay of Pigs Invasion was an unsuccessful action by a CIA-trained force of Cuban exiles to invade southern Cuba, with support and encouragement from the U.S. government, in an attempt to overthrow the Cuban government of Fidel Castro. The conflict was launched in April 1961, less than three months after John F. Kennedy assumed the presidency in the United States. The Cuban armed forces, trained and equipped by Eastern Bloc nations, defeated the invading combatants within three days.

The main invasion landing took place at a beach named Playa Girón, located at the mouth of the bay. The invasion is named after the Bay of Pigs, although that is just one possible translation of the Spanish Bahía de Cochinos. In Cuba, the conflict is sometimes known as La Batalla de Girón, or just Playa Girón.

11 The 1963 "Hotline Agreement" was the first bilateral agreement of the Cold War era between the United States and the Soviet Union, and became the first of a series of growing "confidence building measures" designed to decrease tensions and eliminate the kinds of misunderstandings and miscalculations that could lead to an accidental nuclear war. It was symbolically important, because for the first time, both sides acknowledged that with the advent of nuclear weapons and intercontinental delivery systems, they needed better communication and cooperation to address an entirely new world of different and unprecedented diplomacy and military strategies. Nuclear

weapons had changed both disciplines forever in new and unforeseen ways.

12   The Gulf of Tonkin Incident, or the USS *Maddox* Incident, is the names given to two separate incidents, one disputed, involving North Vietnam and the United States in the waters of the Gulf of Tonkin. On August 2, 1964, the destroyer USS *Maddox*, while performing a DESOTO patrol, was engaged by three North Vietnamese Navy torpedo boats of the 135th Torpedo Squadron. A sea battle resulted, in which the *Maddox* expended over 280 three- and five-inch shells, and which involved the strafing from four USN F-8 Crusader jet fighter bombers. One U.S. aircraft was damaged, one 14.5 mm round hit the destroyer, three North Vietnamese torpedo boats were damaged, and four North Vietnamese sailors were killed and six were wounded; there were no U.S. casualties.

The second Tonkin Gulf incident was originally claimed by the U.S. National Security Agency to have occurred on August 4, 1964, as another sea battle, but instead may have involved the "Tonkin Ghosts," and no actual NVN Torpedo Boat attacks.

The outcome was the passage by Congress of the Gulf of Tonkin Resolution, which granted President Lyndon B. Johnson the authority to assist any Southeast Asian country whose government was considered to be jeopardized by "communist aggression." The resolution served as Johnson's legal justification for deploying U.S. conventional forces and the commencement of open warfare against North Vietnam.

13   The agreement essentially froze the number of strategic ballistic missile launchers at existing levels, operational or under construction, on each side, and permitted an increase

in SLBM launchers up to an agreed level for each party only with the dismantling or destruction of a corresponding number of older icbM or SLBM launchers. In view of the many asymmetries in the two countries forces, imposing equivalent limitations required rather complex and precise provisions.

14   The Paris Peace Accords ending the conflict were signed January 27, 1973, and were followed by the withdrawal of the remaining American troops. The terms of the accords called for a complete ceasefire in South Vietnam, allowed North Vietnamese forces to retain the territory they had captured, released U.S. prisoners of war, and called for both sides to find a political solution to the conflict.

15   The 1973 Chilean coup d'état was a watershed event of the Cold War and the history of Chile. On 11 September 1973, the democratically elected President Salvador Allende was overthrown in a coup d'état organized by the Chilean military and supported by the USA. A military junta took control of the government, composed of the heads of the Air Force, Navy, Carabineros (police force) and the Army led by General Augusto Pinochet. Pinochet later assumed power and ended Allende's democratically elected Popular Unity government.

16   The Yom Kippur War, Ramadan War or October War, also known as the 1973 Arab-Israeli War and the Fourth Arab-Israeli War, was fought from October 6 to 25, 1973, between Israel and a coalition of Arab states led by Egypt and Syria. The war began when the coalition launched a joint surprise attack on Israel on Yom Kippur, the holiest day in Judaism, which coincided with the Muslim holy month of Ramadan. Egyptian and Syrian forces crossed ceasefire lines to enter the Israeli-held Sinai Peninsula and

Golan Heights respectively, which had been captured and occupied since the 1967 Six-Day War. The conflict led to a near-confrontation between the two nuclear superpowers, the United States and the Soviet Union, both of whom initiated massive resupply efforts to their allies during the war.

[17] The Iran–Contra affair was a political scandal in the United States that came to light in November 1986. During the Reagan administration, senior Reagan Administration officials secretly facilitated the sale of arms to Iran, the subject of an arms embargo. Some U.S. officials also hoped that the arms sales would secure the release of hostages and allow U.S. intelligence agencies to fund the Nicaraguan Contras. Under the Boland Amendment, further funding of the Contras by the Reagan administration had been prohibited by Congress.

PARTY CENTRAL

[1] Pick-up sticks is a game of physical and mental skill. A bundle of 'sticks,' approximately six to eight inches long, are held in a loose bunch and released on a table top, falling in random disarray. Each player, in turn, must remove a stick from the pile without disturbing the remaining ones. One root of the name "pick-up sticks" may be the line of a children's nursery rhyme, "...five, six, pick-up sticks!"

[2] Screaming Yellow Zonkers are popcorn with a yellow sugary glaze, in a black box. They were discontinued in 2007.

NERVES OF STEEL AT THE HELM

1   Pan Am was the principal U.S. international air carrier from the late 1920s until its collapse on December 4, 1991. Pan Am was forced to declare bankruptcy on January 8, 1991. Delta Air Lines purchased the remaining profitable assets of Pan Am, including its remaining European routes and the Pan Am Worldport at John F. Kennedy International Airport.

2   For commercial and operational reasons, the airlines had their flights routed through the center corridor whenever possible as this was the shortest of the three air corridors, thereby minimizing the time aircraft spent cruising at ten thousand feet. At such a low altitude, modern jet aircraft could not attain an efficient cruising speed. This extended flight times and increased fuel consumption. Therefore, use of the center air corridor was the most economical option.

3   Tinsel-like strips, similar to the shredded British-designed material called "window" used with great success by R.A.F. and U.S. bombers in World War II to impair the accuracy of Hitler's radar-controlled antiaircraft guns.

EDIE FORGES EAST BERLIN

1   Those with Top Secret Cryptologic Security Clearances with the National Security Agency weren't allowed into the east.

2   Army Headquarters controlling the American Sector for four decades in West Berlin

3   Alexanderplatz is a large public square and transport hub in the central Mitte district of Berlin. Berliners often call it simply Alex, referring to a larger neighborhood stretching from Mollstraße in the northeast to Spandauer Straße and the Rathaus (City Hall) in the southwest. During the 1960s, it was turned into a pedestrian zone and enlarged as part of the German Democratic Republic's redevelopment of the city center. It is surrounded by several notable structures including the Fernsehturm (TV Tower), the second tallest structure in Europe.

BERLIN, THE "ISLAND CITY"

1. The Potsdam Agreement was an agreement on policy for the occupation and reconstruction of Germany and other nations after fighting in the European Theater of World War II had ended with the German surrender of May 8, 1945. It was drafted and adopted by the major victorious powers, the USSR, USA, and UK, at the Potsdam Conference between July 17 and August 2, 1945.

2   The city of Berlin was located some 113 miles behind the "Iron Curtain."

3   Although the blockade had been lifted, restricted air travel over East Germany remained in effect until reunification. Allies were allowed to travel only in the three designated air corridors, one each for British, American, and French aircraft respectively, used during the airlift.

4   An accord reached by each of the major allied powers who were victorious in WWII, namely, the United States, Great Britain, France, and the Soviet Union.

5   A separate West German citizenship did not formally exist; West German authorities considered the pre-war all-German citizenship to continue.

6   The Bundestag ("Federal Diet" or "Lower House of German Parliament") is the parliament of Germany. It was established with Germany's constitution of 1949 (the Grundgesetz), and is the successor of the earlier Reichstag.

7   The Bundesrat ("federal council" or "upper house of German parliament") is the representation of the sixteen Federal States (Bundesländer) of Germany at the federal level. It has its seat at the former Prussian House of Lords in Berlin.

8   The Berlin S-Bahn is a rapid transit system in and around Berlin. It consists of fifteen lines and is integrated with the mostly underground U-Bahn to form the backbone of Berlin's rapid transport system. Unlike the U-Bahn, the S-Bahn crosses the Berlin City and state border into the surrounding state of Brandenburg, mostly from the former East Berlin but today also from West Berlin to Potsdam.

9   Berliner Weisse is a cloudy, sour wheat beer. It is a regional beer from Northern Germany, mainly Berlin, dating back to the 16th century. By the 19th century, Berliner Weisse was the most popular alcoholic drink in Berlin, and seven hundred breweries produced it. By the late 20th century there were only two breweries left in Berlin producing the beer, Berliner Kindl and Schultheiss. The name "Berliner Weisse" is protected in Germany, so it can only be applied to beers brewed in Berlin. However, there are a number of American and Canadian brewers who make a beer in the Berliner Weisse style, and use the name. Mit Schuss Berliner Weisse is typically served in a bowl-shaped glass with a shot of flavored syrup such as raspberry

10   The Border checkpoint Helmstedt–Marienborn, called Grenzübergangsstelle Marienborn (GÜSt) by the German Democratic Republic (GDR), was the largest and most important border crossing on the inner German border during the Cold War. Due to its geographical location, allowing for the shortest land route between West Germany and West Berlin, most transit traffic to and from West Berlin was handled by the Helmstedt-Marienborn crossing. The border crossing existed from 1945 to 1990 and was situated near the East German village of Marienborn at the edge of the Lappwald.

11   Flag Orders or Travel Orders: Required for travel to and from Berlin, travel orders bearing the American Flag at the top and typed in English, German, and Russian with name, rank, nationality, identity document number, destination, etc., and signed by the U.S. Army Commandant. They had to be perfect or travel would be interrupted by the Soviets or East Germans. They could and would stop entire trains for one order being inaccurate.

12   "Strict" in the western world was much different definition than "strict" behind the Iron Curtain. If you violated the rules, you were arrested and detained. There was no appeal, no circumstances in mitigation. Simply, you insulted the Motherland and had to make retribution.

ENCOUNTERS

1   Madurodam is a miniature city located in Scheveningen, The Hague, in the Netherlands. It is a model of a Dutch town on a 1:25 scale, composed of typical Dutch build-

ings and landmarks, as are found at various locations in the country. This major Dutch tourist attraction was built in 1952 and has been visited by tens of millions of visitors ever since. The miniature city was named after Jim Maduro, a law student from Curaçao who fought the Nazi occupation forces as a member of the Dutch resistance and died at Dachau concentration camp in 1945. In 1946, Maduro was posthumously awarded the medal of Knight 4th class of the Military Order of William, the highest and oldest military decoration in the Kingdom of the Netherlands, for the valor he had demonstrated in the Battle of the Netherlands against German troops. His parents donated the capital to start the Madurodam project.

2. A pension hotel is a specific type of "boarding house" in European countries. The term comes from the old French pension, which generally refers to room and board costs. In Europe, the word pension is a term for a cheaper hotel or lodging. A European pension house is often much less expensive than a full-scale hotel, and are more akin to a bed and breakfast, small motel.

3. In the 1960s the U.S. Army adopted a program which allowed private associations to be organized as part of its military recreation program. At some point in the 1960s, a few American sailors founded the American Yacht Club Berlin (AYCB) as a private club under the sponsorship of the Berlin Command. It soon became an integral part of the Wannsee Recreation Center assuming responsibility for Red Cross sailing instruction, organizing regattas, and promoting sportsmanship with Allied (British and French) as well as German sailing clubs.

4. British Kiel Yacht Club came into existence on 11 June 1945. Col. W.G. Fryer, confiscated some yachts of the

"Kieler Yacht-Club" and reopened its club house, where BKYC was established. The Club was formally registered by the Sailing Committee in the Lloyd's register of Yacht Clubs at the beginning of 1946. The General Committee and the members were conscious of the responsibility that they had assumed in taking over the assets of the "Kieler Yacht-Club" formerly being the premiere yacht club in Germany as "Kaiserlicher Yacht-Club." Now the Kiel Training Centre (KTC) is a Services Adventurous Training (AT) center in northern Germany. They run sailing, diving and power boating practical AT courses annually, and a range of shore based courses throughout the year. Kiel is situated in the heart of the Baltic, and offers easy access to a range of superb waters. Each year over one thousand five hundred Servicemen make use of our facilities. Courses are all run to National Governing Body syllabus, the Royal Yachting Association (RYA) for sailing and power boating, and the British Sub Aqua Club (BSAC) for diving.

5   Foul weather clothing.

6   The Skagerrak is a 240 kilometer long strait running between Norway and the southwest coast of Sweden and the Jutland peninsula of Denmark, connecting the North Sea and the Kattegat sea area, which leads to the Baltic Sea.

7   A metal railing around the bow of the boat.

8   The Mirka Class was the NATO reporting name for a class of light frigates built for the Soviet Navy in the mid to late 1960s. The Soviet Designation was Storozhevoi Korabl Project 35 and Project 35-M. The role of these ships was antisubmarine warfare in shallow waters.

9   A snack or light meal.

BWPSBBBT, BOWLING FOR BUSES

1. First built in 1884 by Londoner J.E. Hall as the Cyclic Elevator, the name paternoster (Latin for our father) was originally applied to the device because the elevator is in the form of a loop and is thus similar to rosary beads used as an aid in reciting prayers. Paternosters were popular throughout the first half of the 20th century as they could carry more passengers than ordinary elevators. They were more common in continental Europe, especially in public buildings, than in the United Kingdom. They are rather slow elevators, thus improving the chance of jumping on and off successfully. Today, in many countries the construction of new paternosters is no longer allowed because of the high danger of accidents.

   Five people were killed by paternosters from 1970 to 1993. The elderly, the handicapped and children are the most in danger of being crushed. In 1989, the paternoster in Newcastle University's Claremont Tower was taken out of service after a passenger undertaking an up-and-over journey became caught in the drive chain, necessitating a rescue by the fire service. A conventional elevator was subsequently installed in its place. This accident led to an eighteen-month closedown of all UK paternosters for a safety review, during which additional safety devices were fitted. In April 2006, Hitachi announced plans for a modern paternoster-style elevator with computer-controlled cars and normal elevator doors to alleviate safety concerns.

2. In team play either (a) a pre-designated frame in which the player with the lowest pin count on the first ball buys some type of refreshment; or (b) when all but one of the play-

ers in any frame get strikes; the one not striking buys the refreshments for the others.

WHAT TYPE OF ICE CREAM DO YOU LIKE WITH YOUR HIJACKING?

1   The National Cryptologic School (NCS) is a Cryptologic Training School within the National Security Agency (NSA). It is responsible for designing, developing, and delivering curriculum in cryptology, information assurance, language, and leadership. NCS courses are provided to the civilian and military population of the NSA, as well as the Intelligence Community, the military services, and the Central Security Service (CSS). Many of the courses are accredited by the American Council on Education and the Council on Occupational Education, and are eligible for transfer credits at a variety of educational institutions.

2   In 1981, a LOT Polish Airlines Antonov AN-24 operating an internal scheduled service from Katowice to Gdańsk was hijacked en route and forced to land at Tempelhof. Bernard Pietka, the hijacker, was on military service while taking over the aircraft. He was armed with a grenade and a single-shot pistol. The U.S. military authorities arrested the hijacker on arrival and handed him over to the local police. At that time, he was expected to be sentenced to a five-year prison term under West German law. Following the hijacker's arrest, the U.S. authorities released the aircraft, its crew and all fifty passengers to resume their flight to Gdańsk.

3   These accords had been instigated by the U.S., which was worried about air traffic being diverted to Cuba in those days.

4   Stern's account of the incident and trial appear in his book, Judgment in Berlin, Universe Books, New York (1984).

5   Travemünde is an old seaside resort and Germany's largest ferry port at the Baltic Sea with destinations to Sweden, Finland, Russia, Latvia and Estonia. The lighthouse is from 1539 and the oldest German lighthouse at the Baltic coast. Another attraction of Travemünde is the Flying P-Liner Passat, a museum ship anchored in the mouth of river Trave.

6   Landshut is a city in Bavaria in the southeast of Germany, belonging to both Eastern and Southern Bavaria.

PIRATE INVASION

1   The bridge between West and East Germany where the Russians and Americans traded U2 pilot Francis Gary Powers for master spy Rudolph Abel.

2   A one-hundred-square grid, each grid contained a name of a famous person. Each square was sold for $1.00. The first celebrity to die would earn the person who bought the square $75.00. The remaining $25.00 went into our slush fund.

3   Over the next decade I would encounter nearly two hundred others who claimed to have been on board.

4   The Wasserschutzpolizei (WSP—literally translated "Water Protection Police" in German) is the water police

that patrol the waterways, lakes and harbors of Germany around the clock. The WSP are part of the Landespolizei (State Police).

5   The Pfaueninsel (Peacock Island) is an island situated in the Havel River near the Berlin Wannsee. The island is a popular holiday destination. Until 1689, the glassmaker Johannes Kunckel's glassworks stood on the island. At the time, the island was called Kaninchenwerder (Rabbit Isle). East of the island lies a smaller island named Schwanenwerder (Swan Isle).

In 1793, the then Prussian king Frederick William II acquired the island for the Hohenzollern dynasty and built a menagerie and a zoo there, in which peacocks were also housed. At the end of the 18th century, he commissioned the building of the castle on the Pfaueninsel for Gräfin Wilhemine von Lichtenau.

In the postwar period the Pfaueninsel belonged to the western part of Berlin in the Zehlendorf district, what is now the district of Steglitz-Zehlendorf. The island had largely retained its intended character as an idyll of nature in addition to several free-ranging peacocks, other native and exotic birds can be found in captivity, complemented by a rich variety of flora. The entire island is designated as a nature reserve and since 1990 has been a UNESCO World Heritage Site, along with the castles and parks of Potsdam-Sanssouci and Berlin-Glienicke. The best pictures we have of our children were taken on this island.

6   Persona non grata , literally meaning "an unwelcome person," is a term used in diplomacy with a specialized and legally defined meaning.

RUNAWAY TANK

1. The Bundeswehr (German for "Federal Defense Force") comprises the unified armed forces of Germany and their civil administration and procurement authorities. The States of Germany are not allowed to maintain armed forces of their own, since the Basic Law of Germany states that matters of defense fall into the sole responsibility of the Federal government.

2. The Bundesnachrichtendienst (Federal Intelligence Service, BND) is the foreign intelligence agency of the German government, under the control of the chancellor's office. The BND acts as an early warning system to alert the German government to threats to German interests from abroad.

3. Flak: German, from Fl(ieger) a(bwehr) k(anone), aircraft-defense artillery gun.

4. The Isted Lion (Danish: Istedløven or very archaic name: Flensborgløven), German: Flensburger Löwe or Idstedter Löwe) is a Danish war monument originally intended as a monument of the Danish victory over Schleswig-Holstein in the Battle of Isted (Idstedt) on July 25, 1850—at its time the largest battle in Scandinavian history. Others perceived it more as a memorial for the Danish dead in the battle. Originally erected in Flensburg, Schleswig, it was moved to Berlin by Prussian authorities and remained there until 1945. It was returned to Denmark as a gift from the United States Army and is currently located at Søren Kierkegaards Plads in Copenhagen. A number of politicians have suggested that it be returned to Germany, but the issue remains controversial.

5   The Leibstandarte SS Adolf Hitler (LSSAH) was Adolf Hitler's personal Bodyguard Regiment. The LSSAH independently participated in combat during the Invasion of Poland. The LSSAH was amalgamated into the Waffen-SS together with the SS-VT and the combat units of the SS-TV prior to Operation Barbarossa in 1941. By the end of World War II it had been increased in size from a regiment to a Panzer division. The elite division was a component of the Waffen-SS which was found guilty of war crimes in the Nuremburg Trials.

6   June 30, 1934, known in German history as "The Night of Long Knives," saw fifteen SA (Storm Trooper) Leaders, allegedly involved in the anti-Hitler "Roehm Putsch," executed by SS firing squads on the compound. The execution court yard and surrounding buildings still exist at the corner of Finckensteinallee and Baseler Strasse.

7   It was the M-48 battle tank that was involved in the Checkpoint Charlie standoffs in 1961.

8   Checkpoint Bravo was the name given by the Western Allies to the main autobahn border crossing point between West Berlin and the German Democratic Republic. It was also known as Checkpoint Drewitz-Dreilinden.

GRUPPENREISEN

1   German for group travel.

2   As the Army's primary criminal investigative organization, the U.S. Army Criminal Investigation Command (USACIDC; often referred to as the Criminal Investigation

Division or CID) is responsible for the conduct of criminal investigations in which the Army is, or may be, a party of interest.

3   Berlin's traditional wheat beer is drunk with a schuss, or shot, of either green woodruff syrup or red raspberry syrup in it.

4   German Schnapps is clear, colorless, and has a light fruit flavor.[3] It is distilled from fermented fruit must, is bottled with no added sugar, and normally contains about forty percent ABV.

5   Rigi is a mountain in central Switzerland. It is also known as the "Queen of the Mountains." The highest peak is the Rigi-Kulm at 1,797.5 meters, with Rigi-Hochflue, Dossen and Rotstock and Rigi-Scheidegg being slightly less high.

A PIECE OF THE WALL

1   Along with the S-Bahn (surface train), the U-Bahn (subway) provided citizens with affordable, efficient, public transit.

2   Literally beer bar, Berlin had hundreds ready to slake the prodigious German thirst.

3   Twice brewed, this beer was dark and was once substituted for bread during meals.

4   A thirty-five percent liqueur flavored with herbs.

5   A sweet apple flavored liqueur made from one hundred percent wheat spirit, and blended with apples.

6   On Bernauer Strasse, district Mitte, the houses' walls were the border to the west and people jumped out of their flats into the west in the first days. But soon the windows were walled up, and occupants had to leave their flats. Years later the houses were pulled down.

7   The Volkspolizei (German for "People's Police") was the national police force of the German Democratic Republic (East Germany), whose officers were commonly nicknamed VOPOs.

8   The Ministerium für Staatssicherheit (MfS /Ministry for State Security), commonly known as the Stasi (from Staatssicherheit), was the main security and intelligence organization of the German Democratic Republic (East Germany).

EPILOGUE

1. "Solidarność" is a Polish trade union federation founded in September 1980 at the Gdańsk Shipyard, and originally led by Lech Wałęsa. Solidarity was the first noncommunist party-controlled trade union in a Warsaw Pact country. In the 1980s it constituted a broad anti-bureaucratic social movement. The government attempted to destroy the union during the period of martial law in the early 1980s and several years of political repression, but in the end it was forced to start negotiating with the union.

2. The Securitate was the secret service of Communist Romania. Previously the Romanian secret police was called Siguranța Statului (State Security). Founded on August 30, 1948 with help from the Soviet NKVD, the Securitate

was abolished in December 1989, shortly after President Nicolae Ceaușescu was ousted.

3. The Civic Forum (Czech: Občanské fórum–OF) was a political movement in the Czech part of Czechoslovakia, established during the Velvet Revolution in 1989. The corresponding movement in Slovakia was called Public Against Violence (Slovak: Verejnosť proti násiliu–VPN).

4. The Civic Forum's purpose was to unify the anti-authoritarian forces in Czechoslovakia and to overthrow the communist regime. In this, they succeeded and Václav Havel, its leader and founder, was elected president on December 29, 1989.